The Primary
Decision

Recent Titles in the
Praeger Series in Political Communication
Robert E. Denton, Jr., *General Editor*

The Primary Decision

A Functional Analysis of Debates in Presidential Primaries

William L. Benoit, P. M. Pier,
LeAnn M. Brazeal, John P. McHale,
Andrew Klyukovski, David Airne

Praeger Series in Political Communication

Westport, Connecticut
London

Library of Congress Cataloging-in-Publication Data

The primary decision : a functional analysis of debates in presidential primaries
/ William L. Benoit ... [et al.].
    p. cm. — (Praeger series in political communication, ISSN 1062-5623)
   Includes bibliographical references and index.
   ISBN 0-275-97440-5 (alk. paper)
   1. Primaries—United States. 2. Campaign debates—United States. 3. Presi-
dents—United States—Election. I. Benoit, William L. II. Series.
JK2071.P75   2002
324.273'0154—dc21   2001032925

British Library Cataloguing in Publication Data is available.

Library of Congress Catalog Card Number: 2001032925
ISBN: 0-275-97440-5
ISSN: 1062-5623

First published in 2002

Praeger Publishers, 88 Post Road West, Westport, CT 06881
An imprint of Greenwood Publishing Group, Inc.
www.praeger.com

Printed in the United States of America

The paper used in this book complies with the
Permanent Paper Standard issued by the National
Information Standards Organization (Z39.48-1984).

10 9 8 7 6 5 4 3 2 1

Contents

Series Foreword

Those of us from the discipline of communication studies have long believed that communication is prior to all other fields of inquiry. In several other forums I have argued that the essence of politics is "talk" or human interaction.[1] Such interaction may be formal or informal, verbal or nonverbal, public or private, but it is always persuasive, forcing us consciously or subconsciously to interpret, to evaluate, and to act. Communication is the vehicle for human action.

From this perspective, it is not surprising that Aristotle recognized the natural kinship of politics and communication in his writings *Politics* and *Rhetoric*. In the former, he established that humans are "political beings [who] alone of the animals [are] furnished with the faculty of language."[2] In the latter, he began his systematic analysis of discourse by proclaiming that "rhetorical study, in its strict sense, is concerned with the modes of persuasion."[3] Thus, it was recognized over twenty-three hundred years ago that politics and communication go hand in hand because they are essential parts of human nature.

In 1981, Dan Nimmo and Keith Sanders proclaimed that political communication was an emerging field.[4] Although its origin, as noted, dates back centuries, a "self-consciously cross-disciplinary" focus began in the late 1950s. Thousands of books and articles later, colleges and universities offer a variety of graduate and undergraduate coursework in the area in such diverse departments as communication, mass communication, journalism, political science, and sociology.[5] In Nimmo and Sanders's early assessment, the "key areas of inquiry" included rhetorical analysis, propaganda analysis, attitude change studies, voting studies, government and the news media, functional and systems analyses, technological changes, media technologies, campaign techniques, and research techniques.[6] In a survey of the state of the field in 1983, the same authors and Lynda Kaid found additional, more specific areas of concerns such as the presidency, political polls, public opinion, debates, and advertising.[7] Since the first study, they have also noted a shift away from the rather strict behavioral approach.

A decade later, Dan Nimmo and David Swanson argued that "political communication has developed some identity as a more or less distinct domain of scholarly work."[8] The scope and concerns of the area have further expanded to include critical theories and cultural studies. Although there is no precise definition, method, or disciplinary home of the area of inquiry, its primary domain comprises the role, processes, and effects of communication within the context of politics broadly defined.

In 1985, the editors of *Political Communication Yearbook: 1984* noted that "more things are happening in the study, teaching, and practice of political communication than can be captured within the space limitations of the relatively few publications available."[9] In addition, they argued that the backgrounds of "those involved in the field [are] so varied and pluralist in outlook and approach, . . . it [is] a mistake to adhere slavishly to any set format in shaping the content."[10] More recently, Swanson and Nimmo have called for "ways of overcoming the unhappy consequences of fragmentation within a framework that respects, encourages, and benefits from diverse scholarly commitments, agendas, and approaches."[11]

In agreement with these assessments of the area and with gentle encouragement, in 1988 Praeger established the series entitled "Praeger Series in Political Communication." The series is open to all qualitative and quantitative methodologies as well as contemporary and historical studies. The key to characterizing the studies in the series is the focus on communication variables or activities within a political context or dimension. As of this writing, over eighty volumes have been published and numerous impressive works are forthcoming. Scholars from the disciplines of communication, history, journalism, political science, and sociology have participated in the series.

I am, without shame or modesty, a fan of the series. The joy of serving as its editor is in participating in the dialogue of the field of political communication and in reading the contributors' works. I invite you to join me.

Robert E. Denton, Jr.

NOTES

1. See Robert E. Denton, Jr., *The Symbolic Dimensions of the American Presidency* (Prospect Heights, IL: Waveland Press, 1982); Robert E. Denton, Jr., and Gary

Woodward, *Political Communication in America* (New York: Praeger, 1985; 2d ed., 1990); Robert E. Denton, Jr., and Dan Hahn, *Presidential Communication* (New York: Praeger, 1986); and Robert E. Denton, Jr., *The Primetime Presidency of Ronald Reagan* (New York: Praeger, 1988).

2. Aristotle, *The Politics of Aristotle*, trans. Ernest Barker (New York: Oxford University Press, 1970), p. 5.

3. Aristotle, *Rhetoric*, trans. W. Rhys Roberts (New York: The Modern Library, 1954), p. 22.

4. Dan Nimmo and Keith Sanders, "Inroduction: The Emergence of Political Communication as a Field," in *Handbook of Political Communication*, eds. Dan Nimmo and Keith Sanders (Beverly Hills, CA: Sage, 1981), pp. 11–36.

5. Ibid., p. 15.

6. Ibid., pp. 17–27.

7. Keith Sanders, Lynda Kaid, and Dan Nimmo, eds. *Political Communication Yearbook: 1984* (Carbondale, IL: Southern Illinois University, 1985), pp. 283–308.

8. Dan Nimmo and David Swanson, "The Field of Political Communication: Beyond the Voter Persuasion Paradigm," in *New Directions in Political Communication*, eds. David Swanson and Dan Nimmo (Beverly Hills, CA: Sage, 1990); p. 8.

9. Sanders, Kaid, and Nimmo, *Political Communication Yearbook: 1984*, p. xiv.

10. Ibid.

11. Nimmo and Swanson, "The Field of Political Communication," p. 11.

Preface

We take up two topics here. First, we describe the purpose and scope of our investigation. And second, we sketch our functional approach to political campaign discourse.

PURPOSE OF THIS STUDY

This book applies the Functional Theory of Political Campaign Discourse to a relatively infrequently studied—but still important—campaign message form: presidential primary debates. Our goal is to describe and explain the nature of the discourse in these debates. We obtained transcripts or videotapes of 22 presidential primary debates from 1948 to 2000. Videotapes from 1984 and 1988 were transcribed, and the debates from 1948 to 2000 were subjected to content analysis. We combined these new data with the results of analysis of three primary debates from 1996 (Benoit, Blaney, & Pier, 1998). Accordingly, with new analyses of 22 presidential primary debates added to existing Functional analyses of 3 other primary debates, this study is the most sustained inquiry into the nature of this particular campaign message form.

To accomplish this purpose, we begin by justifying our research topic (Chapter 1). We then describe the method we will utilize to analyze these debates (Chapter 2). Next, several chapters describe the results of our analysis of the early debates (1948, 1960, 1968, 1972) and debates from 1980, 1984, 1988, 1992, and 2000. Finally, we test a variety of hypotheses with the combined data for these 25 primary debates.

A FUNCTIONAL APPROACH TO CAMPAIGN DISCOURSE

Our study employs the Functional Theory of Political Campaign Discourse to analyze these debates (see, e.g., Benoit, 1999; Benoit, Blaney, & Pier, 1998). Political campaign discourse possesses one over-arching goal: to persuade citizens to cast their votes for one candidate instead of for an opponent (of course, a few candidates may campaign to promote an issue as well, but they are not primarily concerned with winning the election). Because these votes are choices between competing candidates, persuasive attempts to solicit votes are inherently comparative. In good times, this means choosing the best among two (or more) good contenders; in bad times, it means picking the lesser of two (or more) evils. Each voter chooses to cast his or her ballot for the candidate who appears *preferable* (compared with the alternatives) on the criteria that are most important to that voter. Which criteria matter the most varies from person to person; however, each citizen votes for the candidate who appears to best fulfill the criteria that are most salient to that particular voter.

This goal of seeming to be the preferred candidate impels political persuaders to disseminate messages intended to make them appear *better* than their opponents. Candidates can have three options (functions) available for convincing voters that they are the better choice. First, they may *acclaim* (produce self-praise of) their positive accomplishments or desirable qualities. Second, candidates can *attack* (criticize) other candidates for their failures or undesirable qualities. Third, if attacked—or perhaps we should say, when attacked—candidates may choose to engage in *defense* (refutations) of criticisms or attacks from other candidates. Each of these message functions has the potential to foster the impression that one candidate is more desirable than opponents. In fact, these three functions work together to act as an informal form of citizen cost-benefit analysis. Acclaims proclaim a candidate's benefits. Attacks reveal an opponent's costs. Defenses reject alleged costs. Together, these functions can provide voters with information that can help determine which candidate is preferable.

The point is not that voters are human computers who assign numeric values to each benefit or cost and perform mathematical calculations to determine which candidate is best; costs and benefits are integrated informally. Furthermore, voters choose to invest varying amounts of time and effort learning about the candidates to make their vote choices. Still, a citizen casts a vote for the candidate who, based on the information available to (and salient to) that voter, has the best mix of costs and benefits.

The basic ideas of the Functional Theory of Political Campaign Discourse have appeared in earlier writings. For example, Smith (1990) noted that "in no other profession [besides politics] do people pursue and defend jobs by publicly boasting and attacking others" (p. 107). Popkin (1994) argued that "each campaign tries hard to make its side look better and the other side worse" (p. 232). Jamieson (1996) observed that "from the country's first contested election, strategists have offered voter advertising that venerated their candidate and vilified his opponents" (p. ix). Thus, acclaiming and attacking are viewed as common features of political campaigns. One of the few sources to acknowledge defense as a third function is Trent and Friedenberg (2000), who observed that political TV spots perform all three of these basic functions: extol the candidates' own virtues; condemn, attack, and question their opponents; and respond to attacks or innuendos.

The Functional Theory divides these utterances (acclaims, attacks, defenses) into two topics: *policy* (issues) and *character* (image or personality). Policy utterances, in turn, are subdivided into remarks that address *past deeds* (laudable accomplishments in acclaims; blameworthy failures in attacks), *future plans* (specific campaign promises, means to an end), and *general goals* (ends). Character comments are subdivided into utterances that address *personal qualities* (e.g., honesty, compassion), *leadership ability* (including experience in office), and *ideals* (basic values or principles).

The categories of policy (issues) and character (image) have been used to investigate television spots before the introduction of the Functional Theory (see, e.g., Joslyn, 1980; West, 1997). However, research on political debates has not tended to use these categories. Nor are the three subdivisions of policy (past deeds, future plans, general goals) and of character (personal qualities, leadership ability, ideals) common topics in the literature.

Acknowledgments

Several people deserve thanks for their contributions, direct and indirect, to this project. First, Bill's wife Pam (Benoit, 1997) wrote the first treatment of acclaiming in the communication literature (and the most extensive treatment of this topic in any discipline). She has been supportive as Chair of the Department of Communication at the University of Missouri. She also permitted him to tie up the TV and VCR for videotaping the seemingly endless 2000 primary debates.

Jennifer Benoit is always an inspiration for Bill. Because she was busy attending college, she didn't watch these debates with him (unlike during the 1996 campaign). It is great to have such a loving, intelligent, and fun daughter. At this writing, she is spending her second year of college studying in Nice, France.

Kurt Ritter, Joe Blaney, and John Morello provided us with videotapes of debates for which transcripts could not be located (Kurt also provided us with a transcript of one primary debate). Kathy Kendall and Goodwin Berquist helped locate transcripts of two early primary debates. Kelly Larson transcribed one of the debates. Mike Stephenson ran the Pearson's r, correlating attacks and defenses. The Web Chi-Square Calculator, developed by Catherine N. Ball and Jeffrey Connor-Linton (http://www.georgetown.edu/cball/webtools/web_chi.html) was very useful. Bill's students in his Presidential Primary Campaign seminar listened patiently while he worked out some of the ideas we develop in this book. Of course, the co-authors have been very important to this study, devoting significant time to this research even as they pursued doctoral degrees and taught courses.

The Primary
Decision

1

Introduction

This chapter begins by developing reasons for studying presidential primary campaigns. Then political debates in particular are justified as objects of study. We then review the scant literature on presidential primary debates. Next, we explain our purpose and the hypotheses driving our analysis. We end by describing the remainder of this work.

WHY STUDY PRESIDENTIAL PRIMARY CAMPAIGNS?

In various sports playoffs, the top team from one conference or league plays the top team from the other division in the championship game. But what if the two best teams in a sport in a given year belong to the *same* division? If one conference is clearly weaker than the other, then the most exciting—and most decisive—game may well be the conference playoff (semifinal), not the championship game. The conference playoffs decide which team gets to face the representative of the weaker conference and, in all probability, determine the ultimate champion.

This situation can arise in presidential campaigns as well as in sports. In 1976, for example, President Gerald Ford did not occupy a strong position. Regardless of whether he was really to blame for the state of the economy, or whether anyone else could have done a better job, he was president when the economy was perceived as weak, and accordingly, he was blamed for the sluggish economy. We will of course never know for certain, but it is distinctly possible that other Democrats besides Jimmy Carter (e.g., Mo Udall) could have defeated Ford in the 1976 general election. Similarly, four years later in 1980 Carter faced not only a struggling economy but the hostage crisis. John Anderson, Howard Baker, George Bush, John Connally, Phil Crane, and Robert Dole all challenged Ronald Reagan for the Republican nomination. Conceivably some (or any) of these candidates could have beaten Carter if they had but won the Republican nomination. The 1980 Republican primary determined that only Reagan would have the opportunity to face Carter, and defeat him, in the general campaign. In 1992, Bush's victory in Operation Desert Storm was fading fast from memory, and once again the economy was perceived as troubled. Jerry Brown, Tom Harkin, Bob Kerrey, and Paul Tsongas challenged Bill Clinton for the Democratic nomination. Perhaps Clinton was not the only Democrat capable of besting Bush in the general election. However, because he won the primaries, Clinton was the one who had the chance to challenge Bush, and he made the best of it. In each of these cases, it is distinctly possible that the primary race ultimately determined who would be president, by deciding who won the right to face a weak opponent. This would make these primary races, in a very important sense, more important than the general campaign.

Furthermore, the mere fact that primaries determine who has the opportunity to run in the general campaign as the party's nominee, with all the partisan support that position legitimizes, makes primaries important. It makes sense that, in a democracy, members of the two key political parties have the right to select their parties' nominees (something they were essentially denied in earlier years, when there were fewer primaries and primary results were not binding on delegates— see, e.g., Davis, 1997, or Kendall, 2000). In short, it matters that Michael Dukakis represented the Democratic Party in 1988, rather than Bruce Babbitt, Dick Gephardt, Al Gore, Jesse Jackson, or Paul Simon. The primaries determined that Bob Dole personified the Republican Party in 1996, not Lamar Alexander, Pat Buchanan, Bob Dornan, Steve Forbes, Phil Gramm, Alan Keyes, Dick Lugar, Arlen Spector, or Morry Taylor. It is important that George W. Bush, rather than John McCain, Steve Forbes, Gary Bauer, Orrin Hatch, or Alan Keyes, represented the Republican Party in 2000—and that Al Gore rather than Bill Bradley exemplified the Democrats. The primaries narrow the field of presidential hopefuls to two principal candidates, determining the choice America faces in the general election.

The need for research into primary campaigns is particularly acute because primaries are quite different from general election campaigns. First, the contenders in primaries belong to the same party. In 2000, for example, Democrat Bill Bradley faced Democrat Al Gore for the right to lead this party in the general campaign. Similarly, Republicans John McCain, Steve Forbes, Alan Keyes, Orrin Hatch, and Gary Bauer all challenged George W. Bush for the Republican nomination. The fact that primary contests are between members of the same party means that political party membership cannot determine the outcome of the primary. Candidates must use other resources, like campaign messages, to sway voters. Voters must make their decisions on bases other than their political party affiliation.

The fact that contenders in the primaries belong to the same party also has implications for the target of attacks in primary races. Republicans battle Republicans, whereas Democrats fight Democrats. Candidates occasionally attack members of the opposing party (particularly front-runners or incumbents running for reelection) in primaries, but their chief focus should be on their immediate opponents, who are their fellow party members. For example, Pat Buchanan in 1992 had the option of attacking President George Bush or one of the Democrats (Brown, Clinton, Harkin, Tsongas) in his primary messages. He chose to focus his attacks on Bush rather than on the Democratic candidates. The situation is quite different in the general election, when loyal party members are expected to support the nominee, and the candidates' attacks focus exclusively on the opposing party's nominee. The resources (ideas, arguments) available to Buchanan for attacks vary according to whether he attacked Bush or Clinton in 1992.

Second, particularly in the early stages of primaries, there can be a multitude of contenders during the primary campaign. For example, in 1996 Lamar Alexander, Pat Buchanan, Bob Dole, Bob Dornan, Steve Forbes, Phil Gramm, Alan Keyes, Dick Lugar, Arlen Spector, and Morry Taylor participated in primary debates. Some of these politicians were longshots, but there were several plausible rivals for the Republican nomination. This situation creates problems for candidates who need to distinguish themselves from (all) opponents and for voters who want to decide which candidate is the best option in a large field. In the general election, however, there are only two principal contenders (although Ross Perot did make things interesting, especially in 1992). The sheer number of contenders makes it more difficult for voters to keep track of candidates and their issue positions during the primaries. It is far easier to draw comparisons between two (or three) general campaign candidates than between six or more primary campaign contenders.

Third, primary races are in a constant state of flux. As some contenders perform poorly in early primaries, they drop out of the race. Other politicians can opt into the primary campaign while it is in progress. In the 2000 race, for example, Elizabeth Dole had entered and already dropped out of the race before Orrin Hatch joined the race for the Republican nomination. Buchanan, a Republican, switched to the Reform Party during the 2000 presidential campaign. The number and identity of candidates can change rapidly as the primary season unfolds. Although Perot dropped out of the 1992 general election and then later returned, typically the general campaign is much less fluid than the primary. These fluctuations increase the difficulty voters have in tracking and comparing candidates during the primary campaign.

A fourth difference between the two campaign phases is that the site of the primary campaign shifts over time. For example, early in the primary season candidates campaign hard in Iowa and New Hampshire (paying a few visits to other states) until the caucus in Iowa and the primary in New Hampshire occur. Once the results for these states are announced, candidates never visit them again during the primaries. Their attention shifts to the next set of primary states, which they will abandon in turn once those elections pass. Voters presumably attend more closely to the primary in their own state (if it has one). In the general election, the candidates criss-cross the country, visiting states (especially those with many electoral voters and states in which the race is close) numerous times throughout the course of the general campaign.

Fifth, the fact that we do not have a simultaneous, national primary system means that the news media places an inordinate emphasis on early primaries, held in states that are not representative of the nation as a whole and have few electoral votes (particularly Iowa and New Hampshire). It also means that results in these early contests have a disproportionate effect on perceived viability of the candidates with voters and campaign donors. In the general election, the states with the most electoral college votes (like California), and the swing states that either candidate could win, are the most important ones. In the primary, in sharp contrast, the date of the primary is one of the most important factors in determining a state's importance.

For example, this means that Iowa and New Hampshire are very important in the primary campaign but relatively unimportant in the general campaign. On the other hand, some states that matter in the general campaign are unimportant in the primaries. Although Bob Dole delayed announcing that he had clinched the nomination in 1996 until after California's primary, in point of fact the primary in California did not affect the outcome (Dole had in fact clinched the Republican nomination before the California primary was held). However, California was an important battleground in the general campaign that year. It was no surprise to learn that in the 2000 campaign California moved its primary to an earlier point in the season.

Thus, primaries are a very important stage of the presidential campaign. They decide which candidates have the best chance to win the general election (the Democratic and Republican Parties' nominees) and which could determine the outcome of the general election if one party is weak. Primaries are distinct from general campaigns in several important ways. Therefore, the need to research this stage of the campaign is particularly important (see, e.g., Davis, 1997; Kendall, 2000).

WHY STUDY POLITICAL DEBATES?

Given that the primary phase of the presidential campaign merits scholarly attention, why do political debates merit scholarly attention? Contenders for the presidency make use of a wide variety of campaign messages. Candidates give dozens or hundreds of stump speeches, distribute pamphlets, air television spots, and appear on interview shows. Recently, candidates have developed Internet sites for promoting their candidacy. In mid-1999, for example, voters could find Web pages for each of the major candidates: Bill Bradley and Al Gore (on the Democratic side) as well as Lamar Alexander, Gary Bauer, Pat Buchanan, George Bush, Elizabeth Dole, Steve Forbes, John Kasich, Alan Keyes, John McCain, Dan Quayle, and Bob Smith (on the Republican side). When Orrin Hatch joined the campaign later, he too added a Web page. However, there are several reasons to consider political debates a particularly important message form.

First, debates have become a routine component of the primary campaign. Hellweg, Pfau, and Brydon (1992) observe that "primary election debates have become an increasingly prevalent feature of the presidential nomination process" (p. 67). In fact, the first presidential debate was a nationally broadcast Republican primary contest between former Minnesota Governor Harold E. Stassen and New York Governor Thomas E. Dewey in 1948. Primary debates occurred in 1952 and 1956 (Best & Hubbard, 2000; Davis, 1997; Kendall, 2000). The most famous presidential debate (keeping in mind that Abraham Lincoln and Stephen Douglas debated during a Senate campaign) pitted Senator John F. Kennedy against Vice President Richard M. Nixon in 1960. However, Kennedy warmed up for the Nixon-Kennedy debates by facing Senator Hubert H. Humphrey in West Virginia just prior to the West Virginia primary. While there was a fairly long hiatus in general debates (no general debates occurred in 1964, 1968, or 1972), primary debates occurred in 1968, 1972, and 1976 before general debates were resumed in 1976 with the Carter-Ford encounters. Thus, many more campaigns have featured primary than general political debates (13, 8). Davis (1997) concluded that "televised primary debates have become an inescapable component of the presidential nominating process. The public has come to expect them" (p. 153). Thus, primary debates are an established and common component of the presidential campaign process.

Furthermore, the number of primary debates has increased rapidly in recent campaigns. During the 1992 election campaign, for example, there were 13 primary and 3 general debates. In 1996, 7 primary and 2 general debates were held. In the most recent election cycle (2000) 22 primary debates and 3 general debates were held in the fall. This proliferation of presidential primary debates provides voters with more opportunities to see the competing candidates. Appendix I lists 92 debates, over four times as many primary as general presidential debates (20 debates have featured the Republican and Democratic nominees for president). Furthermore, because many primary campaigns feature multiple candidates, far more candidates participate in primary than in general election debates.

Second, presidential primary debates provide useful information to voters. Because a vote is a choice between competing candidates, voters must compare the candidates to decide which one is preferable. We do not argue that all voters are rational decisionmakers who seek out as much information as possible and perform explicit cost-benefit analyses of candidates. Particularly in the primary, many voters do not expend a great deal of effort to investigate the candidates. However, there are many primary debates, and some voters do watch them (remember that the main audience for primary debates is composed of members of the candidates' party who are likely to vote, not the entire population). When people are exposed to candidates and their messages, they cannot help but form impressions. Political debates are especially useful campaign messages forms, because voters can learn something about all of the participants' positions on the issues and their character. Debates provide citizens the chance to see the candidates together, discussing the same issues simultaneously (Carlin, 1994; Hellweg, Pfau, & Brydon, 1992; Swerdlow, 1984). Jamieson (1987) explains, "As messages running an hour or longer, debates offer a level of contact with candidates clearly unmatched in spot ads and news segments. . . . The debates offer the most extensive and serious view of the candidates available to the electorate" (p. 28). In political debates, viewers have the opportunity to directly compare and contrast the candidates in an extended period of time.

Another advantage of political debates is that they are more spontaneous than other message forms:

> Voters may obtain a somewhat less contrived impression of the candidates from watching debates than they can get from other kinds of campaign messages, like television spots. While candidates do prepare for the debates, not every question from the panelists, moderators, or audience members can be anticipated; not every remark from an opponent can be anticipated. Furthermore, unlike speeches or television spots with scripts

and teleprompters, candidates are not usually allowed to bring prepared notes to debates. Thus, viewers may get a somewhat more spontaneous and accurate view of the candidates in debates. (Benoit, Blaney, & Pier, 1998, p. 172)

This means that the impression formed of the candidates during political debates may be less contrived than other campaign messages. If so, this means debates are qualitatively better sources of information for voters.

Some scholars remain skeptical of the effects of political debates. Writing about general campaign debates, Jamieson and Birdsell concluded that "debates don't very often convert partisans on one side to the other" (1988, p. 161; see also Swerdlow, 1984). However, in the primary phase partisanship cannot possibly decide the outcome of the campaign, because all candidates in a given race belong to the same party. Republicans must obtain information to select among the array of Republican candidates, just as Democratic voters must learn about the candidates to decide which Democratic candidate to support. Primary debates are therefore an important source of information that can help partisans select a nominee.

It is important to note that primary debates may have more impact on voters than general election debates. The contenders are generally less well known to voters in the primaries than in the general campaign. Hellweg, Pfau, and Brydon (1992) explained that primary debates can have substantial influence on voters: "Primary and caucus debates exert considerable influence on the acquisition and development of voter perceptions about the personal characteristics of candidates precisely because they occur early in a political campaign, prior to the development of initial impressions and/or the hardening of perceptions about the candidates" (p. 122). Of course, there are potential difficulties with or limitations on primary debates. Some primary debates, particularly early in the campaign, may feature 10 or more candidates. It is difficult for voters to come away from such confrontations with a clear understanding of every contender. Still, such debates provide them an opportunity to learn more about the candidates who interest them the most. They occur at a point in the campaign where the opportunity to exert influence on beliefs and attitudes may be highest.

There is relatively little research on presidential primary debates. However, what research is available suggests that primary debates are capable of influencing voters. Experimental studies indicate that those who watch primary debates learn about the candidates and their issue positions (Benoit, McKinney, & Stephenson, in press; Benoit & Stephenson, 2000; Best & Hubbard, 2000; Lanoue & Schrott, 1989; Pfau, 1987; Yawn, Ellsworth, Beatty, & Kahn, 1998). Martel (1983) argued that debates can make a difference: "It is doubtful that Jimmy Carter could have risen from a 2 percent recognition factor to win the Democratic nomination without his performance in the 1976 candidates forums. Similarly, John Anderson's campaign might never have gotten off the ground in 1980 had he not distinguished himself in the Iowa Republican forum" (p. 52). Orren (1985) asserted that primary debates in Illinois, Pennsylvania, and New York affected primaries in 1984. Pfau (1987) argued that "the 1984 intraparty debates influenced viewer attitudes about Hart and Jackson; [although] they produced only a slight change in attitude toward Mondale" (p. 694). Thus primary debates have the potential to influence voters. There is ample justification for an extended investigation into this important message form.

LITERATURE REVIEW

Five studies offered a historical or critical view of a particular primary debate. Ray (1961) discussed the 1948 Dewey-Stassen radio debate. Berquist (1960) and Stelzner (1971) examined the 1960 Kennedy-Humphrey debate. The 1968 Kennedy-McCarthy debate was treated by Murphy (1992). Blankenship, Fine, and Davis (1983) discussed the 1980 Republican primary debates. Additionally, three studies concerned the effects of debate format (Kane, 1987; Pfau, 1984, 1988). None of these studies are designed to quantify the functions of topics of these debates.

Two studies performed content analysis on presidential primary debates. Hellweg and Phillips (1981) studied the 1980 Houston Republican primary debate. Although they also performed a visual analysis of this debate, given our approach, the verbal analysis is more relevant for present purposes. They divided candidate utterances by turns (answers or rebuttals). Most candidate utterances (Bush, 94%; Reagan, 81%) included a direct statement of policy. Bush attacked (made a statement about an opponent's position) more than Reagan (67% to 42%). Both included evidence (Reagan, 46%; Bush, 39%), emotional appeals (Bush, 56%; Reagan, 31%), historical references (Bush, 61%; Reagan, 31%), and factual illustrations (Reagan, 50%; Bush, 39%) in many statements. There was some use of humor (Bush, 39%; Reagan, 11%) and less use of analogies (Reagan, 12%; Bush, 6%). A limitation of their method is that we know how many statements contained these items but not whether they were major emphases or minor components.

Benoit, Blaney, and Pier (1998) employed the Functional Theory of Political Campaign Discourse to analyze three 1996 primary debates. Unlike most research in this area, they use the theme (idea or argument; defined in Chapter 2) as their coding unit. They found that acclaims

(54%) outnumbered attacks (38%), which in turn were more frequent than defenses (9%). These debates involved only Republicans (Clinton was not challenged in the Democratic primary process), and more attacks targeted other Republicans (58%) than were directed toward Clinton and the Democrats (17%) or the establishment (25%). More utterances addressed policy (58%) than character (42%). They also concluded that Dole was one of the candidates who frequently addressed the topics that were most important to voters (along with Alexander and Forbes).

Thus, we have some insight into the nature of presidential primary debates. However, it is limited to four debates in two campaigns. Clearly this does not provide an adequate understanding of this important campaign message form.

PURPOSE

This study applied the Functional Theory of Political Campaign Discourse to 22 presidential primary debates: 1 debate from each of 1948, 1960, 1968, and 1972; 3 debates from each of 1980, 1984, 1988, and 1992; and 3 Republican and 3 Democratic debates from 2000 (Benoit, Blaney, & Pier, 1998, analyzed 3 primary debates from 1996, and that data will be integrated into the new results). We will test 18 hypotheses developed out of the existing research on the Functional Theory of Political Campaign Discourse (Benoit, 1999; Benoit, Blaney, & Pier, 1998, 2000; Benoit & Brazeal, 1999; Benoit & Harthcock, 1999b; Benoit, Pier, & Blaney, 1997; Benoit & Wells, 1996; Benoit, Wells, Pier, & Blaney, 1999).

We will divide our hypotheses into three groups. Some primarily concern the Functional Theory of Political Campaign Discourse, some pertain to these debates as part of the primary campaign, and some relate to these campaign messages as debates.

Functional Theory Hypotheses:

H1. Acclaims will outnumber attacks, which in turn will outnumber defenses.
H2. More utterances will discuss policy than character.
H3. Attacks will be positively related to defenses.
H4. More acclaims than attacks will occur on general goals and ideals.

Primary Campaign Message Hypotheses:

H5. Attacks will be less frequent in primary than in general debates.
H6. Defenses will be less frequent in primary than in general debates.

H7. Acclaims will be more frequent in primary than in general debates.

H8. There will be less emphasis on policy and more on character in primary than in general debates.

H9. Fewer past deeds and more general goals will occur in primary than in general debates.

H10. Past deeds will be used to attack more and acclaim less in primary than in general debates.

H11. Candidates will attack their own party more than the other party.

H12. More attacks will target the front-runner than other candidates.

H13. Front-runners will attack the other party more than other candidates.

Campaign Debate Hypotheses:

H14. Defense will be more frequent in primary debates than in TV spots.

H15. Attacks will be more frequent in primary TV spots than in debates.

H16. Acclaims will be less frequent in primary debates than in TV spots.

H17. Debates will discuss policy more and character less than will TV spots.

When we test these hypotheses on the entire data set, in Chapter 9, we will explain why we made these particular predictions. However, it suffices at this point to explain the kinds of questions we will be exploring in our analysis of presidential primary debates. Empirical tests of these 17 hypotheses will substantially enhance our understanding of presidential primary debates.

OUTLINE OF THE WORK

Chapter 2 will explain the method and procedures employed to analyze these debates. This will be followed by descriptive chapters that present the results of our content analysis of primary debates from the four early years (1948, 1960, 1968, 1972), 1980, 1984, 1988, 1992, and six primary debates from 2000. Chapter 9 will test the 17 hypotheses described above on the entire body of data (adding in the data on three 1996 primary debates from Benoit, Blaney, & Pier, 1998) and discuss those results. Appendix I lists primary debates, identifying the ones included in our sample. Appendix II provides an example of an acclaim and an attack on each of the three forms of policy and three forms of character taken from our sample of primary debate texts.

2

Method and Procedures: Analyzing Acclaims, Attacks, and Defenses

In this chapter, we begin by describing the texts we used for our analysis. Then we explain the Functional Theory of Political Campaign Discourse, which guided this study. Next we describe the procedures used to content-analyze the texts. Finally, we report figures for intercoder reliability of our content analysis.

TEXTS

We obtained transcripts of 22 primary debates. We located one primary debate transcript from each of four early campaigns (1948, 1960, 1968, and 1972). We also obtained three transcripts from each campaign from 1980 through 1992 (3 primary debates from 1996 were analyzed in Benoit, Blaney, & Pier, 1998). Because it was timely, and because both political parties had contested primaries, we analyzed 3 Republican and 3 Democratic primary debates from the 2000 campaign. Transcripts of 1980 debates were found in Reuter (1983). Three debates each from 1984 and 1988 were transcribed for this study from videotapes. Transcripts of 3 primary debates from 1992 and 6 from 2000 were obtained from the World Wide Web via Lexis-Nexis. This gives us new data from 22 primary debates, spanning 1948 to 2000, to add to data from three 1996 debates that have already been analyzed. Appendix I provides a list of every primary debate that we located or was mentioned in the literature (Best & Hubbard, 2000, were very useful in creating this appendix).

FUNCTIONAL THEORY OF POLITICAL CAMPAIGN DISCOURSE

The Functional Theory of Political Campaign Discourse was employed to analyze these primary debates (Benoit, 1999; Benoit, Blaney, & Pier, 1998, 2000; Benoit & Brazeal, in press; Benoit & Harthcock, 1999b; Benoit, Pier, & Blaney, 1997; Benoit & Wells, 1996; Benoit, Wells, Pier, & Blaney, 1999). This theory holds that citizens vote for the candidate who appears *preferable* on whatever criteria are most salient to each individual voter. Candidates have but three options to increase their apparent preferability. First, they may *acclaim*, or engage in self-praise (see Benoit, 1997). The better one candidate appears to voters, the more likely that candidate will be preferred over opponents. Second, candidates may *attack*, or reduce an opponent's desirability (Benoit & Dorries, 1996; Benoit & Harthcock, 1999a; Benoit & Wells, 1996). Because voting is a comparative judgment, a successful attack makes the opponent appear worse to voters, giving the attacker a net gain in preferability (of course, an unsuccessful attack can backfire and damage the source of the attack). Third, if attacked, an opponent may engage in *defense*, refuting accusations to restore lost preferability (Benoit, 1995). So a candidate has these options to persuade voters that he or she is preferable to opponents.

These three functions—acclaims, attacks, defenses—can occur on two broad topics, *policy* and *character*. Policy concerns government action and problems amenable to government action, whereas character concerns the traits, properties, or qualities of the candidates. Each of these two topics has three subdivisions. Policy can be divided into past deeds (usually taken in elective office), future plans (campaign promises), and general goals (ends). Character can be split into personal qualities (human traits), leadership ability (experience), and ideals (principles or values). Appendix II provides an illustration of an acclaim and an attack on each of these topics from the debates analyzed in this study.

This theory is compatible with other approaches to understanding voting. Past deeds provide information for voters who prefer retrospective voting (What have you done for me?). Discussion of future plans and general goals assists voters who practice prospective voting (What will you do for me if you are elected?). These three subtopics together (past deeds, future plans, general goals) are helpful for voters who decide their vote choice more on policy (issues) than on character (image). On the other hand, the three forms of character utterances—personal qualities, leadership ability, and ideals—appeal to voters who tend to base their vote on character rather than policy. Partisanship comes into play in this analysis as well, especially in ideals and general goals (e.g., Republicans are often seen as the better party for controlling inflation, whereas Democrats are usually seen as the better party for fighting unemployment; Popkin, 1994). Thus, the Functional Theory of Political Campaign Discourse corresponds to other approaches to understanding voter behavior.

PROCEDURES

The categorical content analytic procedure employed in this study had six steps. First, discourse was unitized into themes, which are utterances that address a coherent idea. Berelson (1952), for example, defined a theme as "an assertion about a subject" (p. 18). Holsti (1969) explained that a theme is "a single assertion about some subject" (p. 116). A theme can also be conceptualized as an argument (argument₁; see O'Keefe, 1977) about the candidates. Second, the function of each theme was then categorized according to these rules:

Acclaims are themes portraying the candidate in a favorable light.

Attacks are themes portraying the opposing candidate in an unfavorable light.

Defenses are themes responding to (refuting) an attack on the candidate.

Third, the target of each attack was identified. Normal targets included the other members of the party of the debate (e.g., George W. Bush at times attacked John McCain or Steve Forbes in 2000 primary debates). When the target was a member of the party debating, the candidate frequently was a participant in the debate. However, in the 2000 campaign, Bush was attacked in the debates he did not attend (this also happened, for example, to Dole in 1996). The other party, and its presumed nominee, was another common target of attack. In the most recent campaign, Democrats frequently attacked Bush (and other Republicans), and Republicans often criticized Gore. The establishment or status quo (often conceptualized as politicians of either party who live and work in the Washington, DC, "beltway") was also attacked. Other targets of attack were relatively uncommon (e.g., communism and the Communist Party were frequently attacked in the 1948 primary debate). For debates that occurred in 1980 and after, we used Lexis-Nexis Academic Universe to locate public opinion polls to identify which candidate was the front-runner at the time of each debate.

Fourth, each theme was classified as concerning policy or character according to these rules:

Policy themes address government action or problems amenable to such action.

Character themes address characteristics, traits, abilities, or attributes of the candidates.

Fifth, policy themes were broken down into past deeds, future plans, and general goals, whereas character themes were analyzed into personal qualities, leadership ability, and ideals (as noted above, each of these is illustrated in Appendix II).

Finally, policy themes were coded according to issue addressed. Again using Lexis-Nexis Academic Universe (for debates in 1980 and after), we located a public opinion poll identifying which issues were most important to voters prior to the debates. We used the top five issues (more if several issues were tied for fifth) for each debate as the categories for this analysis.

INTERCODER RELIABILITY

Six coders analyzed the data, and intercoder reliability was calculated using one entire debate (this debate was not included in the analysis). Cohen's *kappa* (1960) was calculated to control for possible agreement due to chance. *Kappa* for function (acclaims, attacks, defenses) varied from .77 to .97 among the six coders. *Kappa* for topic (policy, character) ranged from .68 to .82. *Kappa* for form of policy (past deeds, future plans, general goals) varied from .71 to .89. *Kappa* for form of character (personal qualities, leadership ability, ideals) ranged from .65 to 1.0. *Kappa* for target of attack varied from .75 to .94. Fleiss (1981) explains that "values [of *kappa*] greater than .75 or so may be taken to represent excellent agreement beyond chance. . . and values between .40 and .75 may be taken to represent fair to good agreement beyond chance" (p. 218). Thus, even though six different coders analyzed these debates, we considered intercoder reliability to be acceptable (88% of the values we obtained were excellent and 12% were good; the mean value for *kappa* for each of these coding decisions was excellent according to Fleiss).

SAMPLE TEXTUAL ANALYSIS

To illustrate our content analysis procedures, we provide an excerpt from the February 21, 2000 Democratic Debate at the Apollo Theater in New York City. Each theme is numbered in this transcript and the coding of that theme is presented after that number.

> BRADLEY: One of the first things I would do is I would give 10,000 scholarships a year at $7,500 a year scholarship to people who after four years would agree to teach in an urban or rural school district in the areas of computer science, math, science or foreign languages [1 Acclaim, Policy,

Future Plan, Education]. We need teachers in our communities who understand these subjects and have the equipment [2 Acclaim, Policy, General Goal, Education].

The next thing I would do is something I call info-stamps, which empowers those who don't have to be able to get the equipment and the software that they need in order to be a part of the digital revolution. We have food stamps. We need info-stamps to be able to accomplish this objective [3 Acclaim, Policy, Future Plan, Education]. And in terms of education, I think—and you mentioned race in education—I think it is important to know that in 1980, '81 and 1979 there was an issue before the Congress that related to whether the—whether the government would provide tax-exempt status to schools that racially discriminate. Al Gore supported those measures, and I'd like to know today why [4 Attack, Policy, Past Deed, Education, Gore (target)].

SHAW: Mr. Vice President, one minute.

GORE: Well, I made a speech last week on how to close the digital divide. I'll deal with this briefly and then respond to Bill's false charge [5 Attack, Character, Personal Quality, Bradley (target)]. I believe that we need to get computing centers in the community for children and for adults, and we need to finish connecting every classroom and library to the Internet. We need to get computers in the schools [6 Acclaim, Policy, General Goal, Education], and we need to train the teachers [7 Acclaim, Policy, General Goal, Education]. We cannot allow a digital divide to exacerbate the gap between rich and poor [8 Acclaim, Character, Ideal].

Now, as for this false charge—two in a row. First of all, on government procurement, there was no change there [9 Defense, Policy, Simple Denial, Education]. That's a false charge [10 Attack, Character, Personal Quality, Bradley (target)].

Secondly, look, you have misrepresented that vote entirely, Senator Bradley [11 Attack, Character, Personal Quality, Bradley (target)]. That was not about affirmative action. That was about quotas [12 Defense, Policy, Differentiation]. It was 337 members of the Congress voted against that. You voted for—the same way on final passage [13 Attack, Character, Personal Qualities, Bradley (target)].

Now, let me—let me talk about a more recent vote. Not 20 years ago. In 1995, you were the only Democratic senator . . .

SHAW: Time.

GORE: . . . to vote against affirmative action to help expand the number of African-American-owned broadcasting outlets—radio stations and TV stations. Why did you—why were you the only Democratic senator on the Finance Committee to vote against that [14 Attack, Policy, Past Deed, Racial Equality, Bradley (target)]?

STATISTICAL ANALYSIS

Rather than test each hypothesis for each debate (or even for each campaign), we decided to run one set of statistical analyses on the entire data set, reported in Chapter 9. Given that most of our data are nominal (categorical) data, most hypotheses will be tested with *chi-squares*. However, two hypotheses (H3, H12) require Pearson's *r* to correlate the frequency of attack and of defense and the frequency of attacks on candidates with positions in the polls.

3

Early Primary Debates: 1948, 1960, 1968, 1972

As noted earlier, the institution of primary debates was initiated in the 1948 Republican primary, in which Thomas Dewey challenged Harold Stassen. We were also able to obtain transcripts of three other early debates. This chapter will present the results of our analysis of the four early debates we obtained for this study: 1948 (Dewey-Stassen), 1960 (Humphrey-Kennedy), 1968 (Kennedy-McCarthy), and 1972 (Humphrey-McGovern). Each section (campaign) will begin with some brief background material. Then functions, topics, and target of attack will be discussed (we were unable to locate public opinion polls about the most important issue for voters in these debates, so we omitted that analysis in this chapter).

1948: DEWEY-STASSEN

Franklin D. Roosevelt was elected to his fourth term as president in 1944. When he died in April 1945 (in the third month of his new term), his vice president, Harry S. Truman, became president. Truman was the one who ordered the atomic bomb used in Japan. Although this meant he was president when World War II ended, he also had to supervise the changeover from a wartime to a peacetime economy. Truman called Congress into a special session in July 1948 to consider economic reforms. They did not enact his proposed reforms, but that gave him a scapegoat to blame for America's economic problems. The Republicans won control of both houses of Congress in the 1946 midterm elections, and many thought Truman could not win in 1948 (Splaine, 1995). The famous photograph of President Truman holding a newspaper with the headline announcing his "defeat" at Dewey's hands is from this campaign.

The first presidential primary debate in history occurred on May 17, 1948, in Portland, Oregon (5/17/48, OR). Republicans Harold E. Stassen upheld the affirmative, and Thomas E. Dewey the negative, on the question "Should the Communist Party in the United States be outlawed?" This historic clash was broadcast on the Mutual Broadcasting System radio network.

This debate has attracted relatively little attention from scholars. Ray (1961) concluded that "Dewey must be adjudged the more effective of the two debaters," reported that Dewey won the Oregon primary, and noted, "There can be little doubt the Oregon victory (in the face of great odds [against Dewey; one poll gave Stassen a 70% to 30% margin] at the outset of the Oregon primary) greatly enhanced his prestige and did serious damage to Stassen's bid for the nomination" (p. 266). Of course, Dewey went on to win the Republican Party's nomination, although he lost a close race to Harry Truman in the general campaign.

Functions of the 1948 Debate

Acclaims (51%) were the most common function in this debate. For example, Stassen acclaimed the following general goal: "to keep America and other free countries strong in a military sense" (5/17/48, OR). Similarly, Dewey asserted, "My interest in is preserving the country from being destroyed by the development of an underground organization" (5/17/48, OR). Thus, acclaims were common in this encounter. See Table 3.1.

Attacks were the next most common function, at 44%. Stassen attacked Dewey's claims that we have adequate laws against communism and that all we need is to enforce them: "May I ask then why it is that the Communist party organization has been growing so strong in New York" (5/17/48, OR), the state of which Dewey is governor. This statement functions to attack Dewey's failure to act against communism in his own state (past deeds). Dewey in turn attacked Stassen's suggestion that we outlaw communism, calling it "a violation of the Constitution of the United States and of the Bill of Rights. . . . [I]t is immoral and

TABLE 3.1
Functions of the 1948 Dewey-Stassen Debate

	Acclaims	Attacks	Defenses
Dewey	29 (45%)	33 (52%)	2 (3%)
Stassen	39 (57%)	25 (36%)	5 (7%)
Total	68 (51%)	58 (44%)	7 (5%)

nothing but totalitarianism itself" (5/17/48, OR). Attacks were another frequent kind of utterance in this confrontation.

Defenses were relatively uncommon, at 7% of the utterances in this debate. For example, after Stassen attacked Dewey because of the large number of communists in Dewey's state, the governor replied: "Now we have a lot of communists in New York; we have a great many of them, and they cause us great trouble. But we lick them. The number is down from 100,000 two years ago to 70,000 last year to 68,000 this year. In New York their influence is at the lowest ebb in their history" (5/17/48, OR). Here, given his inability to deny the problem, he worked to minimize it instead. Stassen replied to Dewey's attack on his proposal to outlaw communism in the United States with this defense: "This is not a matter of outlawing any ideas. It is not a matter of any thought control" (5/17/48, OR). Dewey used denial to reject Stassen's attack. Thus, while uncommon, defenses did occur in these debates.

These functions were not used in the same proportions by each debater: Dewey had more attacks (52%) than acclaims (45%). This means that Stassen, the front-runner at the time, was the target of more attacks than the trailing candidate. This also means that the front-runner, Stassen, engaged in more acclaiming (57%) than attacking (36%).

Topics of the 1948 Debate

Together, these candidates discussed policy (48%) roughly the same amount as they talked about character (52%). Dewey focused more on character (61%), whereas Stassen concentrated on policy (58%). For example, Stassen identified numerous general goals in this utterance:

> Avoiding inflation booms with their out-of-reach prices, preventing depression crashes with unemployment, widely developing the superb natural resources of water, forests, and minerals, constantly improving housing and health, establishing a fair balance between capital and labor, assuring to agriculture a fair share of the national income, advancing in civil rights, decreasing discrimination and bigotry, and constantly endeavoring to win happier homes throughout America. (5/17/48, OR)

These goals may appear to be somewhat outside the scope of the proposition (outlawing the Communist Party) but may well have appeared desirable to listeners. Dewey acclaimed his openness, a personal quality: "I have talked directly to the people of my views and invited their questions and welcomed any opportunity to meet with others in a joint discussion" (5/17/48, OR). Thus, both policy and character were topics of discussion in this debate. See Table 3.2.

TABLE 3.2
Policy vs. Character in the 1948 Dewey-Stassen Debate

	Policy	Character
Dewey	24 (39%)	38 (61%)
Stassen	37 (58%)	27 (42%)
Total	61 (48%)	65 (52%)

Neither candidate attacked the Democratic Party. Policy utterances were allocated fairly equally between past deeds (30%), future plans (38%), and general goals (33%). For example, Stassen acclaimed his past success in dealing with communists. In "Minneapolis, we found that we could make progress if we cooperated with the Federal government, the state government and the local government. . . . [W]e gradually weeded them out" (5/17/48, OR). This passage lauds a past deed. Dewey attacked Stassen's (future) plan of outlawing the Communist Party: "Illegalization has not proved effective in Canada and other countries which tried it" (5/17/48, OR). Stassen explained that one of his "principal objectives" was "to keep America and other free countries strong in a military sense" (5/17/48, OR). He does not specify the means that would be used to accomplish this objective, which makes this utterance a general goal. Thus, each candidate employed all three forms of policy. See Table 3.3.

Neither candidate discussed leadership ability in this debate. Character utterances were divided roughly between personal qualities (52%) and ideals (48%). For instance, Dewey spoke of his "optimism," a personal quality. Stassen argued that a president should have "courage and [willingness to] sacrifice, and . . . intelligence and realism," and he implied that he possessed those traits (5/17/48, OR). Dewey acclaimed his ideals when he praised "ideals and moral standards and justice." Similarly, Stassen proclaimed his belief in "complete constitutional rights and liberties in America" (5/17/48, OR). These passages illustrate the nature of character comments in this debates.

TABLE 3.3
Forms of Policy and Character in the 1948 Dewey-Stassen Debate

	Policy						Character					
	Past Deeds*		Future Plans		General Goals		Personal Qualities		Leadership Ability		Ideals	
Dewey	3	0	1	17	3	0	7	16	0	0	15	0
Stassen	1	14	4	1	14	3	9	2	0	0	11	5
Total	4	14	5	18	17	3	16	18	0	0	26	5
	30%		38%		33%		52%		0%		48%	

*Acclaims/attacks.

Target of Attack in the 1948 Debate

Dewey and Stassen focused their attacks on each other (79%). Given the topic of the debate—the Communist Party—it was not surprising to see Stassen attack the communists almost as much as he attacked Dewey. For example, Stassen declared, "These communist organizations are not really political parties, they are actually fifth columns, they are quisling cliques" (5/17/48, OR). Dewey criticized his opponent's understanding of the situation: "Mr. Stassen has not adhered to his subject or his statements. He says he is for the Mundt bill because, says Mr. Stassen, it outlaws the Communist Party. But the fact of the matter is, he is in grievous error. . . Mr. Mundt, whose bill it is, says his bill does not outlaw the Communist Party" (5/17/48, OR). This passage functions to reduce Stassen's credibility on the topic of the debate.

Stassen, who was the front-runner at this point, was the target of attack more often than was Dewey (33 attacks on Stassen to 13 attacks on Dewey). Neither candidate attacked the opposing party, the Democrats, or Truman, the incumbent president and likely nominee. See Table 3.4.

Conclusion

As noted earlier, Dewey won the Republican nomination. Truman, who had become president when Franklin D. Roosevelt died in office, won the election. Truman had a 4.5% margin in the popular vote and a 114 electoral vote margin (Splaine, 1995). This campaign saw the inauguration of presidential primary debates, which would grow over time until in 2000 there were 22 presidential primary debates.

1960: HUMPHREY-KENNEDY

Eisenhower had been president from 1952 through 1960. The economy appeared to be in relatively good shape, but there was growing concern about the communist threat. Richard Nixon was the vice president, and he was nominated to represent the Republican Party. However, Democratic senators Hubert Humphrey and John Kennedy were the principal contenders during the still abbreviated (and nonbinding)

TABLE 3.4
Target of Attack in the 1948 Dewey-Stassen Debate

	Communists	Opponent
Dewey	0	33 (100%)
Stassen	12 (48%)	13 (52%)
Total	12 (21%)	46 (79%)

primary season. Two other senators, Lyndon Johnson and Stuart Symington, hoped to compete for the Democratic nomination at the convention (Splaine, 1995).

Humphrey and Kennedy faced one another just before the West Virginia primary in Charleston on May 3, 1960 (5/3/60, WV). At this time in our nation's history it was not necessary to run in primaries to win the party's nomination. In fact, eight years later Humphrey would secure the Democratic nomination without winning or campaigning in a single primary (Levine, 1995). However, Kennedy wanted to prove to party bosses that he—a relatively youthful and Catholic senator from the Northeast—could appeal to voters in the Protestant South. He chose to challenge Humphrey in seven states, including West Virginia. Best and Hubbard (2000) report that Kennedy also debated Lyndon Johnson, Kennedy's eventual running mate, in California in July, although we were unable to locate video or text from that encounter.

Functions of the 1960 Debate

This debate focused more on acclaims (71%) than attacks (26%) or defenses (3%). For instance, Kennedy acclaimed this future plan: "I think the Defense Department should set aside of every contract a percentage which would go into those areas where there was a high level of unemployment" (5/3/60, WV). In contrast, Humphrey attacked the Eisenhower-Nixon administration: "The Republican administration has put on the brakes on the American economy" (5/3/60, WV). When it was suggested that the Democratic Congress had failed to help West Virginia, Kennedy denied that accusation: "I remember that—taking the lead in Defense Manpower Policy No. 4 in 1953 to steer defense contracts into distressed areas" (5/3/60, WV). Table 3.5 shows the distribution of the functions in this debate.

Topics of the 1960 Debate

This debate had a tendency to emphasize policy (60%) over character (40%). Kennedy, for example, attacked the past deeds of the current administration: "The President can veto programs, as this administra-

TABLE 3.5
Functions of the 1960 Kennedy-Humphrey Debate

	Acclaims	Attacks	Defenses
Kennedy	63 (79%)	14 (18%)	3 (4%)
Humphrey	62 (64%)	32 (33%)	3 (3%)
Total	125 (71%)	46 (26%)	6 (3%)

tion has done—housing, water pollution, unemployment compensation" (5/3/60, WV). Humphrey indicted the lack of leadership in the current administration, chastising "a conservative Republican government in Washington that is content with standing still in a changing America and a very rapidly changing world" (5/3/60, WV). Thus, both candidates discussed policy and character issues, as Table 3.6 reveals.

The candidates allocated their policy remarks fairly evenly, with 38% of themes discussing past deeds, 29% future plans, and 32% general goals. For example, Humphrey lamented the "considerable recession in the country, growing unemployment, and genuine economic distress" (5/3/60, WV). These are past deeds (failures) blamed on the present administration. Kennedy suggests his plan to direct some Pentagon purchasing, a future plan that offers a means for helping areas suffering from high unemployment. Humphrey focuses more on ends than means in acclaiming these general goals: "The next President" must "develop a force for peace," "feed the hungry," "heal the sick," and "teach the illiterate" (5/3/60, WV). Thus, these candidates used a variety of policy utterances in this debate. See Table. 3.7.

When the candidates addressed character topics, they focused more on personal qualities (46%) than leadership ability (28%) or ideals (26%). Kennedy reveals a personal quality when he admits that "I think it would be a mistake and misleading to suggest that I'm going to favor a good many of the programs that I've talked about earlier . . . and at the same time say that I'm going to reduce income taxes this year. I don't think that is possible" (5/3/60, WV). While ostensibly discussing policy, this passage reveals his honesty, his unwillingness to promise everything to everyone. Humphrey attacked the leadership of Nixon and the Republicans in this debate: "Richard Nixon must not be the next President of the United States. We've had too many years of caretaker government that ignores problems and avoids opportunities, too many years of shameful neglect of America's needs at home, and waste and loss of Americans' prestige abroad. We have, in fact, been the victims of a "no go—go slow—not now—veto administration" (5/3/60, WV). Kennedy explained that our country "was founded on the principle of

TABLE 3.6
Policy vs. Character in the 1960 Kennedy-Humphrey Debate

	Policy	*Character*
Kennedy	44 (57%)	33 (43%)
Humphrey	58 (62%)	36 (38%)
Total	102 (60%)	69 (40%)

The Primary Decision

TABLE 3.7
Forms of Policy and Character in the 1960 Kennedy-Humphrey Debate

	Policy					Character					
	Past Deeds*		Future Plans		General Goals		Personal Qualities		Leadership Ability		Ideals	
Kennedy	1	11	17	1	14	0	16	2	9	0	6	0
Humphrey	6	21	12	0	17	2	11	3	5	5	11	1
Tota	7	32	29	1	31	2	27	5	14	5	17	1
	38%		29%		32%		46%		28%		26%	

*Acclaims/attacks.

religious freedom" (5/3/60, WV). This passage acclaims one of Kennedy's ideals. These passages illustrate Kennedy's and Humphrey's use of character topics in this debate.

Target of Attacks in the 1960 Debate

Kennedy and Humphrey spent over five times as many utterances attacking the opposition party (85%) than one another (15%). For instance, Humphrey declared, "The Republican administration has put the brakes on the American economy" (5/3/60, WV), clearly attacking the Eisenhower/Nixon administration. Similarly, Kennedy noted that "in this administration, particularly the credit policies and all the rest, have worked to their [small business's] disadvantage" (5/3/60, WV). The two Democratic candidates were the target of virtually the same number of attacks (Kennedy was attacked four times by Humphrey; Humphrey was attacked three times by Kennedy). These excerpts show how character utterances were employed in this debate. These data are displayed in Table 3.8.

Conclusion

Kennedy was selected as the Democratic nominee; fellow senator and Texan Lyndon B. Johnson was Kennedy's running mate. In an extremely close election, Kennedy defeated Nixon by 118,574 popular votes (0.2%)

TABLE 3.8
Target of Attack in the 1960 Kennedy-Humphrey Debate

	Democratic Opponent	Republicans/Nixon
Kennedy	3 (21%)	11 (79%)
Humphrey	4 (12%)	28 (88%)
Total	7 (15%)	39 (85%)

but a larger 84 electoral vote margin (Splaine, 1995). Unfortunately, Kennedy was assassinated on November 22, 1963, whereupon Johnson assumed the presidency. Johnson, along with Vice President Hubert Humphrey, defeated Barry Goldwater in 1964.

1968: KENNEDY-McCARTHY

Johnson was the president in 1968, having become president after Kennedy was assassinated and defeating Barry Goldwater in 1964. However, on March 31, after the New Hampshire primary, he announced he would not seek reelection, almost certainly because of the escalating war in Vietnam and a performance in the New Hampshire primary that was less strong than expected. Two Democratic senators met again to debate in 1968, this time in California on June 1, 1968 (6/1/68, CA). Robert F. Kennedy debated Eugene J. McCarthy on ABC's *Issues and Answers*. Tragically, Kennedy was shot three days later in Los Angeles (Splaine, 1995). Vice President Hubert Humphrey, who did not campaign in the primaries, was selected to be the Democratic nominee. This divisive convention in Chicago led to key reforms in the primary system.

Functions of the 1968 Debate

Once again acclaims predominated in this primary debate: 61% of themes were acclaims, 29% were attacks, and 11% were classified as defenses. For example, McCarthy explained that "I think everyone feels that we need better police forces now, that there ought to be more Federal money given to the state and local authorities so that we could have more policemen and more patrolmen" (6/1/68, CA). In contrast, Kennedy attacked a proposal he attributed to McCarthy: "I would be opposed to what I understand Senator McCarthy's position of forcing a coalition government on the Government of Saigon, a coalition with the Communists, even before we can begin negotiations" (6/1/68, CA). However, McCarthy denied that he favored such an action, defending against this attack: "I didn't say I was going to force a coalition government on South Vietnam" (6/1/68, CA). Table 3.9 displays the functions of this debate.

TABLE 3.9
Functions of the 1968 Kennedy-McCarthy Debate

	Acclaims	Attacks	Defenses
Kennedy	71 (63%)	37 (33%)	4 (4%)
McCarthy	56 (58%)	23 (24%)	18 (19%)
Total	127 (61%)	60 (29%)	22 (11%)

Topics of the 1968 Debate

These candidates focused more of their comments on policy (64%) than character (36%). Kennedy attacked the establishment when he discussed tax policy: "There are dozens of people in the United States who make more than $200,000 a year who pay no taxes at all. There are dozens of people who make more than a million dollars a year who pay no taxes at all" (6/1/68, CA). McCarthy acclaimed his leadership ability based on his service in the Senate: "I'm on the Foreign Relations Committee. . . . The Foreign Relations is security which a President has to have in order to run the foreign policies of this country" (6/1/68, CA). Table 3.10 presents the data on the topics of the utterances in this debate.

These candidates tended to stress their general goals (51%, mostly acclaims) more so than past deeds (31%, mostly attacks) or future plans (18%). Kennedy explained that the United States ought not interfere in the internal affairs of another country: "I'm opposed under those circumstances, to sending American soldiers in, because I don't think we can be the policemen of the world and straighten out every problem all over the globe" (6/1/68, CA). Discussing domestic policy, McCarthy declared that "we need better police forces now" (6/1/68, CA). Both of these suggestions are put forth as desirable ends (general goals) rather than specific means (plans). Kennedy attacked the present system, arguing that "we have 14 million Negroes who are in the ghettos at the present time. We have here in the State of California one million Mexican-Americans whose poverty is even greater than many of the black people" (6/1/68, CA). Clearly poverty among minority groups was a problem at the time of the debate. In order to implement his goal of improving the police forces, McCarthy proposed that "there ought to be more Federal money given to the states and local authorities so that we could have more policemen and more patrolmen" (6/1/68, CA). This offers the means (a future plan) for accomplishing his goal. Thus, the candidates used all three forms of policy, although general goals were most common. See Table 3.11.

The utterances that address character in this debate focused on leadership ability (62%) more than personal qualities (20%) or ideals (18%). For instance, Kennedy touted his experience when he noted that "I was

TABLE 3.10
Policy vs. Character in the 1968 Kennedy-McCarthy Debate

	Policy	Character
Kennedy	76 (70%)	32 (30%)
McCarthy	50 (56%)	39 (44%)
Total	126 (64%)	71 (36%)

TABLE 3.11
Forms of Policy and Character in the 1968 Kennedy-McCarthy Debate

	Policy						Character				
	Past Deeds*		Future Plans		General Goals		Personal Qualities		Leadership Ability		Ideals	
Kennedy	3	19	9	7	36	2	4	5	13	3	6	1
McCarthy	4	13	5	2	25	1	2	1	17	5	3	1
Total	7	32	14	9	61	3	6	6	30	8	9	2
	31%		18%		51%		20%		62%		18%	

*Acclaims/attacks.

a member of the National Security Council for three and a half years" and "as Attorney General I was the chief law enforcement officer" (6/1/68, CA). His background qualifies him to lead the nation as president. McCarthy stated that "I'm on the Foreign Relations Committee," giving him foreign policy credentials. He also explained that "there's two committees you got to have in order to really run the country very well. You have to have the support and response of the Finance Committee and the Ways and Means Committee in the House. . . . I served on it [the Finance Committee] for four years" (6/1/68, CA). This service shows that McCarthy also has domestic leadership experience. An example of a statement concerning personal qualities occurred when Kennedy accused McCarthy of "distortion of the record," questioning McCarthy's honesty (6/1/68, CA). Kennedy also illustrated the use of ideals when he declared, "I love my country but I love it in justice" (6/1/68, CA). Clearly, the ideals of both patriotism and justice can be seen in this statement. Thus, these passages illustrate Kennedy's and McCarthy's use of character topics in the debates.

Target of Attack in the 1968 Debate

In this debate, Kennedy and McCarthy attacked the establishment more often (73%, although they never attacked their Republican opponent by name)—than each other (27%). McCarthy was attacked about twice as often by Kennedy (11 times) as McCarthy attacked Kennedy (5 times). For instance, Kennedy accused McCarthy of "distortion of the record" (6/1/68, CA). McCarthy suggested that his opponent would not provide "real leadership" (6/1/68). Kennedy also attacked the establishment when he lamented, "We cut twenty-five million from the Head Start program, which is going to mean a thousand students already in the Head Start program here in the state of California will be excluded, 4,000 in the state of Mississippi" (6/1/68, CA). These data are displayed in Table 3.12.

TABLE 3.12
Target of Attack in the 1968 Kennedy-McCarthy Debate

	Opponent	Other Party	Establishment
Kennedy	11 (30%)	0	26 (70%)
McCarthy	5 (22%)	0	18 (78%)
Total	16 (27%)	0	44 (73%)

Conclusion

Neither Kennedy nor McCarthy won the Democratic nomination in 1968. Vice President Humphrey, who did not campaign or win in any of the primaries, was chosen to lead the party. Former Vice President Nixon and former Democrat and now American Independent candidate George Wallace vied with Humphrey in the general election. Nixon won with less than 1% more of the popular vote than Humphrey but 110 electoral college votes more than Humphrey (Splaine, 1995).

1972: HUMPHREY-McGOVERN

Nixon was the Republican incumbent in 1972. The economy appeared to be strong, although there was a growing deficit. Nixon traveled to both China and Russia, moves that strengthened his approval ratings. However, the conflict in Vietnam that had damaged Johnson in 1968 haunted Nixon four years later. On May 8, Nixon ordered Haiphong Harbor (and other ports) to be mined, increasing concerns about this war. In June, the Democratic National Campaign headquarters was burglarized, and Nixon denied any administration involvement (Splaine, 1995).

The final early debate we analyzed once again featured two Democratic senators, one also a former vice president. Hubert H. Humphrey and George McGovern debated on May 28, 1972 in California (5/28/72, CA). Best and Hubbard (2000) observe that these candidates debated three times in California, including once with Shirley Chisholm, George Wallace (who was injured in May and represented in the debate by a surrogate), and Sam Yorty. Again, we were only able to locate video or text of one debate.

Functions of the 1972 Debate

This debate emphasized acclaims and attacks equally (44%), although Humphrey attacked more than McGovern (53% to 33%). McGovern acclaimed his tax proposal: "Every American who is earning $12,000 a year or less would profit from the proposal that I have suggested"

(5/28/72, CA). On the other hand, Humphrey repeatedly attacked his immediate opponent, McGovern, declaring that

> Senator McGovern is wrong on Israel. Senator McGovern has been wrong on unemployment compensation. Senator McGovern has been wrong on labor law and on the two or three great issues here in California; on his massive unrealistic and I think rather outside welfare program, he is wrong. On taxation he is contradictory and inconsistent. He is wrong on defense cuts. I think they will cut into the muscle, in the very fiber of our national security. (5/28/72, CA)

McGovern replied to some of these attacks, providing a defense against them: "As to my position on Israel, I see no essential difference between the views that I held and the view that Senator Humphrey holds. . . . As we move along, I will comment on welfare and taxation and defense" (5/28/72, CA). Thus, these candidates employed these functions in their debate. These data appear in Table 3.13.

Topics of the 1972 Debate

These candidates emphasized policy (78%) more than character (22%). McGovern discussed his policy proposals: "I am the one candidate that has outlined a program to provide a job for every worker in this country and I have said where the money is going to come from. I have pointed out where we are going to get additional revenues, by closing some of the tax loopholes. I have pointed out where waste can be reduced in the military establishments, and then that money invested in job creating enterprises" (5/28/72, CA). In the next passage, Humphrey touted his leadership ability: "I have the experience as a mayor, as a senator, as a vice president" (5/28/72, CA). Both candidates discussed policy as well as character in this debate. The data on topic are reported in Table 3.14.

These candidates, who belonged to the challenger party, focused policy themes on future plans (48%), with past deeds at 36% and general goals at 15%. For example, Humphrey criticized his opponent's future plans: "Let me say a $72 billion welfare proposal that Senator McGovern

TABLE 3.13
Functions of the 1972 McGovern-Humphrey Debate

	Acclaims	Attacks	Defenses
Humphrey	42 (42%)	53 (53%)	5 (5%)
McGovern	37 (46%)	26 (33%)	17 (21%)
Total	79 (44%)	79 (44%)	22 (12%)

TABLE 3.14
Policy vs. Character in the 1972 McGovern-Humphrey Debate

	Policy	Character
Humphrey	77 (81%)	18 (19%)
McGovern	47 (75%)	16 (25%)
Total	124 (78%)	34 (22%)

makes today is not only a horrible mess, it would be an unbelievable burden upon the taxpayers" (5/28/72, CA). Humphrey also attacked McGovern's past deeds: "There is no doubt he spoke out against it [involvement in Vietnam] but he voted for it. That is the record. And when it comes to unemployment compensation, he did not vote to support it. He voted against it. When it comes to labor legislation, he voted against it" (5/28/72, CA). McGovern identified this foreign policy objective: "We have to do whatever is necessary to secure the defense of Israel" (5/28/72, CA). Because he does not identify the means, this is an example of a general goal. These passages illustrate the candidates' use of policy comments. See Table 3.15.

These candidates also discussed character during the debate. Character discussion focused on personal qualities (47%), leadership ability (32%), and ideals (21%). For instance, McGovern said that his campaign would "restore some measure of truthfulness and openness in the councils of government" (5/28/72, CA). Telling the truth and being open are desirable personal qualities. Humphrey explained that "I have the experience as a mayor, as a senator, as a vice-president. I have the experience of Congress" (5/28/72, CA). This background sheds light on his leadership ability. McGovern provided an example of ideals when he revealed his "reverence for life and liberty and pursuit of happiness" (5/28/72, CA). These excerpts illustrate the candidates' use of character topics in this debate.

TABLE 3.15
Forms of Policy and Character in the 1972 McGovern-Humphrey Debate

	Policy						Character					
	Past Deeds*		Future Plans		General Goals		Personal Qualities		Leadership Ability		Ideals	
Humphrey	13	15	10	30	7	2	4	6	5	0	3	0
McGovern	5	13	14	6	9	1	4	2	2	4	3	1
Total	18	28	24	36	16	3	8	8	7	4	6	1
	36%		48%		15%		47%		32%		21%	

*Acclaims/attacks.

Target of Attack in the 1972 Debate

Most of the attacks from Humphrey and McGovern were aimed at one another (81%), with a few directed toward Nixon and the Republicans (14%) or the establishment (5%). McGovern was the target of almost four times as many attacks (51) as Humphrey received (13). For example, Humphrey attacked his opponent's position on unilateral troop reductions:

> I do not believe in a unilateral troop reduction, for example, in Western Europe of a hundred fifty thousand, which Senator McGovern has proposed. I believe we ought to negotiate that out with the Russians just like we have negotiated out the ABM freeze, and just like we have negotiated an interim agreement on offensive weapons. You cannot negotiate with the Russians from a position of weakness; if we haven't learned that, we learned nothing. (5/28/72, CA)

However, at times they attacked the Nixon administration. Humphrey declared, "The economy is in disarray. The American people have great doubts about many of the policies of this administration" (5/28/72, CA). Similarly, McGovern said that "people are sick and tired of a war that never ends, which President Nixon has not ended" (5/28/72, CA). These data are reported in Table 3.16.

Conclusion

McGovern won the Democratic nomination in 1972. This is attributable in part to his intimate knowledge of the new rules for allocating primary delegates, which were now bound to primary candidates at the convention (he cochaired the McGovern-Frasier Reform Commission; Davis, 1997). This campaign featured McGovern changing running mates in midstream (Eagleton to Shriver) and the Watergate break-in, which would assume dramatic proportions in 1974. However, Nixon won every state but Massachusetts (and DC) and was reelected. Nixon recycled some of the arguments against McGovern employed by Humphrey in this debate (e.g., welfare reform, defense cuts).

TABLE 3.16
Target of Attack in the 1972 McGovern-Humphrey Debate

	Democratic Opponent	Republicans/Nixon	Establishment
Humphrey	51 (96%)	2 (4%)	0
McGovern	13 (50%)	9 (35%)	4 (15%)
Total	64 (81%)	11 (14%)	4 (5%)

CONCLUSION

We can see some consistency across these four debates. First, no debate had more attacks than acclaims (acclaims were either the most frequent function or tied with attacks). In every debate (and for every candidate) defenses were the least common function. Two individual candidates did use more attacks than acclaims: Dewey in 1948 and Humphrey in 1972.

A second finding is that, overall, these debates focused more on policy than character. Only one candidate dwelled more on character than policy: Dewey in 1948. Dewey's emphasis on character meant that the 1948 debate focused somewhat more on character (52%) than policy (48%). However, from that point forward, every debate and every candidate focused more utterances on policy than character.

In these debates, no form of policy received less than 15% of the comments that were devoted to policy. Past deeds were the most consistent policy topic, receiving between 30% and 38% of policy utterances. Future plans varied from 18% to 48% of the policy remarks. General goals also varied quite a bit, from 15% in 1972 to 51% in 1968. The three forms of character all varied widely. Personal qualities ranged from 20% to 52%, leadership ability varied widely from 0% to 62%, and ideals fluctuated from 18% to 48%.

In 1948 Stassen only attacked the communists (never Dewey). This could have bolstered his reputation among those who despised the Communist Party, but these attacks did nothing to reduce the apparent desirability of his opponent. In 1960, both (John) Kennedy and Humphrey targeted more of their attacks to Nixon than to each other. Similarly, in 1968, both (Robert) Kennedy and McCarthy attacked the establishment more than one another. In 1972, however, Humphrey and McGovern themselves were the most common target of attack. There was no consistent pattern, then, in target of attack.

Presidential primary debates (indeed, presidential debates in any phase) were completely new in 1948 and did not start to proliferate until 1980. Thus, candidates were developing this new campaign message. Given the fact that primaries were not binding before the changes initiated after the 1968 election, it is not surprising that primary debates were relatively uncommon.

4

1980 Republican Primary Debates: "I Paid for This Microphone!"

It is particularly important to study the 1980 Republican primary because 17% of voters stated that they made their final presidential vote choice during the primaries that year (CBS News/*New York Times*, 1980a). This means that a substantial number of voters paid attention to the primaries and that the process of the primaries affected their voting preferences. This chapter will briefly describe the format of each of the debates; each of the candidates will then be discussed briefly. Finally, the results of this analysis will be presented and illustrated.

BACKGROUND OF THE 1980 REPUBLICAN DEBATES

Through mid-December of 1979 Reagan was considered the front-runner for the Republican Party (Davis, 1997; Pomper, 1981). However, after the Iowa debate in which Reagan refused to participate, Bush closed the gap and positioned himself as a favorite in the public opinion polls. The official reason for Reagan's decision was that he believed intraparty debates tended to split the party (Davis, 1997; Pomper, 1981). Some suggested that Reagan wanted to conserve his resources early in the campaign, especially since he already enjoyed a substantial lead (Abramson, Aldrich, & Rohde, 1982). After the Iowa debate (1/5/80, IA), Bush emerged as a front-runner threatening Reagan's position (Nelson, 1989). Then Reagan agreed to participate in the debates. Following the Nashua debate (2/23/80, NH), Reagan reestablished his position as the frontrunner (Davis, 1997; Pomper, 1981). The South Carolina debate (2/28/80, SC) further solidified Reagan's position.

The Iowa debate included Anderson, Baker, Bush, Connally, Crane, and Dole. Reagan chose not to participate but did agree to meet Bush in the Nashua, New Hamphire, debate. The New Hampshire debate in Nashua is well known because—despite the fact that the campaign managers agreed that this debate would feature just Bush and Reagan— four other candidates showed up to participate. Bush adamantly refused to participate in what he felt was an ambush. In response, Reagan grabbed the microphone and pronounced that he was the one paying for that debate, it was his microphone, and he should be the one making the rules (Abramson, Aldrich, & Rohde, 1982). The moderator, John Breen, disqualified the other four candidates so that a debate between the two front-runners could take place. As the result of media coverage of these events, Bush was perceived as a poor sport, and his candidacy never recovered. Participants in the South Carolina debate included Baker, Bush, Connally, and Reagan.

The remainder of this chapter offers findings of the functional elements of the 1980 Republican primary. The focus is on functions, topics, targets of attacks, and issues addressed by the candidates.

FUNCTIONS OF THE 1980 REPUBLICAN DEBATES

Overall this was a rather positive primary campaign with fully three-quarters of the utterances being acclaims. For example, Bush declared: "We must strengthen the triad. We must strengthen the Navy. I'm in favor of the concept of a three-ocean Navy. Only by being able to project conventional force are we going to deter Soviet aggression" (2/23/80, NH). Each sentence in this passage acclaims Bush's general goal of building a strong defense. While he does not give specific plans of

TABLE 4.1
Functions of the 1980 Republican Debates

	Acclaims	Attacks	Defenses
Anderson	48 (69%)	22 (31%)	0
Baker	89 (74%)	24 (20%)	7 (6%)
Bush	326 (83%)	42 (11%)	24 (6%)
Connally	97 (61%)	58 (36%)	4 (3%)
Crane	56 (89%)	7 (11%)	0
Dole	75 (91%)	7 (9%)	0
Reagan	196 (65%)	99 (32%)	9 (3%)
Total	887 (75%)	259 (22%)	44(3%)

action for strengthening our defense capability, each utterance focuses on an objective that should resonate with the voters. See Table 4.1.

Following acclaims, 259 attacks (22%) were the second most frequent function in these debates. One example of attack was Connally's criticism of the Carter decision to impose an embargo on the sale of grain to the Soviet Union: "Well, first, I don't think the Iowa farmers should pay the price for the failure of the Carter foreign policy. That, that's number one. Secondly, unless the President has a specific agreement with Canada, Australia, and Argentina that they're not going to rush in and fill the void what we're leaving by the failure to sell 17 million metric tons of grain to the Soviet Union, then I think the President's made a mistake" (1/5/80, IA). In this example, Connally launched two very strong attacks against Carter. One attack is for making Iowa farmers pay for the mistakes in foreign policy, and another is for not making sure that other countries do not go against U.S. policy and take advantage of the situation.

Finally, 44 defenses (3%) comprised the smallest portion of these utterances. Bush's utterances presented more than half (24) of the defenses in these debates. One example of these defenses was used by Bush to respond to the suggestion that there were financing problems possibly connected to the Watergate scandal: "I received, as did thirteen other Senate candidates, money from the White House in 1970, long before Watergate. To the best of my knowledge, every single penny of that was reported in accordance with the law" (2/23/80, NH). This utterance was intended to defuse the situation by denying the accusation of wrongdoing.

Individually, each candidate followed the same distribution of utterances—the bulk of the utterances were acclaims, followed by attacks (approximately one-third of the themes), and defenses constituted the smallest percentage of utterances. Anderson, who participated only in one of the debates under review, used 69% acclaims and 31% attacks. Baker, who was included in two debates, employed 74% acclaims, 20% attacks, and 6% defenses. Bush, the only candidate who participated in all three of the debates analyzed here, utilized 83% acclaims, 11% attacks, and 6% defenses. Connally, who participated in two debates, used 61% acclaims, 36% attacks, and 3% defenses. Crane and Dole both participated only in one debate and had nearly identical distribution of utterances with about 90% acclaims and approximately 10% attacks. Finally, Reagan—the front-runner during most of the campaign—participated in two debates and employed 65% acclaims, 32% attacks, and 3% defenses.

While overall the individual distributions followed the total distribution of the percentages, there were some exceptions. Reagan, for example, was the most negative of the candidates: Despite participating in only two of the three debates we analyzed, he advanced the highest number of attacks (99) of all of the candidates in the 1980 primary and the second highest percentage of the attacks (32%). Connally had the highest percentage of attack utterances (36%), but only 58 attacks. To illustrate their use of attacks, consider this statement from Reagan: "But what I think the Republican Party has to do today is recognize that the Democratic party for years has humiliated and demeaned those people [African Americans] by saying the only way to approach them is by an offer of more government handouts" (2/28/80, SC). In this example, Reagan indicts the Democratic Party for making demeaning attempts to deal with the African American community. These excerpts illustrate the three functions that occurred in these primary debates.

TOPICS OF THE 1980 REPUBLICAN DEBATES

In the three debates examined in this chapter, candidates devoted almost twice as many utterances to policy (65%) as to character (35%). This distribution demonstrates that the 1980 Republican primary campaign was primarily focused on the issues of public policy, revealing how the candidates are different in their views from one another and from the incumbent administration. Bush's acclaim is an example of a policy utterance: "I would be active in supporting local law enforcement" (2/23/80, NH). This example provides a glimpse of Bush's ideas for community policing. An example of a character utterance is Bush's acclaim of his ideals: "It's the conviction that I feel about this country. The optimism, the idealism" (2/28/80, SC). As an individual, Bush acclaims his his optimism and idealism. See Table 4.2.

Under the forms of policy, general goals comprised a plurality (42%) of the utterances, with 257 utterances devoted to acclaims and 53 to attacks. Here is an example of an acclaim of general goals by Reagan:

TABLE 4.2
Policy vs. Character in the 1980 Republican Debates

	Policy	Character
Anderson	38 (54%)	32 (46%)
Baker	70 (62%)	43 (38%)
Bush	243 (66%)	125 (34%)
Connally	100 (65%)	55 (35%)
Crane	33 (52%)	30 (48%)
Dole	48 (58%)	34 (42%)
Reagan	212 (72%)	83 (28%)
Total	744 (65%)	402 (35%)

Well, I agree with the things that have been said about fiscal responsibility and cutting government spending. And this can be done, because I think there's enough fat in the federal government today that if you rented it, you could wash the world by making soap out of it. But I believe there has to be even more than a plan of that. We've got to stop the printing press money that is flooding us with this imitation money, lowering the value of our savings and our insurance and so forth. (2/28/80, SC)

This example demonstrates how a candidate can make a statement about policy that is too vague to be easily targeted by an attack. In this example, Reagan acclaimed his goal of battling inflation. Who could reject that goal? In contrast, the next excerpt is an example of attack on Carter's past deeds by Bush: "Under this administration, we sometimes have failed to keep our strategic commitments" (2/23/80, NH). This statement criticized the current administration's foreign policy for compromising American strategic commitments. See Table 4.3.

Past deeds also comprised a significant number of the policy utterances (38%), with a slim majority of those devoted to acclaims (147) and a somewhat smaller number devoted to attacks (136). An example of an acclaim on past deeds is Baker's statement that "I have a consistent record of the support of major civil rights legislation that has come before us since I've been there" in the Senate (2/28/80, SC). In this excerpt, Baker acclaimed his voting record (past accomplishments) in the U.S. Senate on the civil rights legislation.

However, it is also important to note that the most attacks in any single category occur in the area of past deeds (136). An example of such an attack comes from Anderson targeting Reagan: "And I must confess to this audience that I am not a younger Ronald Reagan, with experi-

TABLE 4.3
Forms of Policy and Character in the 1980 Republican Debates

	Policy					Character					
	Past Deeds*		Future Plans		General Goals		Personal Qualities		Leadership Ability		Ideals	
Anderson	4	10	13	6	5	0	3	0	1	1	22	5
Baker	15	16	9	4	25	1	6	3	3	0	31	0
Bush	44	17	46	4	119	13	60	4	26	3	31	1
Connally	20	38	10	3	28	1	3	6	13	10	23	0
Crane	8	7	12	0	6	0	5	0	1	0	24	0
Dole	18	5	12	1	12	0	3	1	14	0	16	0
Reagan	38	43	20	7	62	38	49	4	22	2	6	0
Total	147	136	122	25	257	53	129	18	80	16	153	6
	38%		20%		42%		36%		24%		40%	

*Acclaims/attacks.

ence. I am younger, yes. But I do not share his view of the world. He was opposed to the SALT II agreement, even before the invasion of Afghanistan. He was opposed to the Panama Canal treaties" (1/5/80, IA). In this statement Anderson separated himself from Ronald Reagan and then attacked Reagan's public record. Specifically, Anderson attacked Reagan's objections to the U.S. international agreement to limit strategic armaments and Reagan's opposition to treaties over the Panama Canal.

Future plans were the least likely forms to be discussed in the policy realm. Although they made up 20% of all policy utterances, the vast majority of those were dedicated to acclaims, 122 to 25 attacks. A clear example of an acclaim on future plans can be found in this passage from Bush: "I don't want to see the deficit worse. And so what I've been proposing is a supply-side, an investment-oriented tax cut, every facet of which goes to increased investment, goes to increased savings, so we have more investment in housing, for example" (2/23/80, NH). Here George Bush acclaims his tax-cut plan, which should help him if accepted by the voters, in his bid for Republican nomination. At times these candidates attacked the future plans of other candidates, as did Baker:

> Speaking as we were a moment ago of the proposed grain embargo of sales to the Soviet Union by President Carter: the family farm, more than any other group, would be devastated by such an action, if in fact it is carried out. I think such an action, the embargo of grain sales to Russia, is inhumane, I think it's inappropriate to our foreign policy, and I think it would be destructive to the family farm in this country. (1/5/80, IA)

This is an attack on the decision by the Carter administration to impose a grain embargo on sales to the Soviet Union, which, allegedly, substantially hurt the American farmers and is incompatible with the best interests of America in foreign policy. Such an attack may help the candidate, as it simultaneously should improve the candidate's image with Republican primary voters.

Under forms of character, there was more consistency among the three message forms (personal qualities, leadership ability, and ideals). Ideals took the lead at 40% of the overall total. Baker demonstrated one of the more passionate pleas on ideals: "I believe in America. And I believe that we will have before us an opportunity to do things that no nation has ever dared to dream of. And I believe this election in 1980 may very well be a crossroads time in America's history, when we decide such things as whether or not we have the will and the determination to stay strong" (1/5/80, IA). In this quotation, Baker affirmed his faith in the strengths of America and the ability of the American people to overcome the hurdles of history like an economic crisis facing the country then. This is a good example of a statement that is very difficult to disagree with or to criticize. Attacks on ideals are uncommon. One example can be found in this excerpt when Anderson launched an attack against Reagan: "He takes a view of the economy that I think pretty much goes back to the time of Adam Smith's invisible hand. He doesn't see a genuine role for the federal government when it comes to the causes of advancing human rights, or civil rights, in this country" (1/5/80, IA). This very harsh criticism suggests that Reagan's views on human rights are outdated and that he does not value the causes that Americans embrace.

Personal qualities was the second most commonly addressed character issue, at 36%. In this passage, Baker acclaimed his personal qualities: "I am a fallible mortal. And, as such, yes, there are many things that I've said, as we all have, without thinking and reflecting properly, that we'd like to take back" (1/5/80, IA). In this statement, Baker acclaimed himself as a humble and honest person. This is a typical affirmation of one's good character, which, if accepted, could improve a candidate's favorability with the voters. Attacks on personal qualities can also occur. This excerpt is interesting, because Baker uses varying stands on a policy question (energy price controls) to make the argument that President Carter is inconsistent: "President Carter started out as a candidate for deregulation and decontrol. Then he changed his mind and went for controls at very high prices. And then he changed his mind again" (1/5/80, IA). Notice that this particular statement never suggests which policy is preferable: The point of the attack is that Carter as a person is inconsistent.

Finally, leadership ability received the least attention from the candidates, at 24%, which is still a substantial percentage. It appears, though, that those candidates with the most experience (Bush, Connally, Dole, Reagan) talked the most about it. A good example of acclaiming one's own leadership ability comes from Reagan:

Well, I think that I've had some experience, too. When George said CIA: I was on the presidential commission investigating the CIA almost as long as he was director of it. I was 8 years—we're talking about the top executive government position in the land. Well, for eight years, I was in the second top executive position in the land, governor of the largest and most populous state, California. And by coincidence, incidentally, California, if it were a nation, would be the seventh ranking economic power in the world. I, too, have had contact with the leaders of state of over 20 nations, in those countries and in my own state. And the state I took over was in the same shape the federal government is in today: on the verge of bankruptcy. . . . I've had the executive experience that comes closest to what would face the president of the United States. (2/28/80, SC)

This is a very clear statement that Reagan believed in his qualifications. Reagan stated that his experience in providing oversight to the Central Intelligence Agency (CIA) matched that of George Bush in directing it, his closest rival for the nomination. Also, Reagan stated that his experience as a governor prepared him well for the presidency, because both are executive positions. That assertion is supported by an analogy to California as comparable to substantial world economic powers, which could grant credibility to its governor as a world-class economic leader.

On the other hand, Anderson was not shy about attacking the leadership ability of Jimmy Carter: An excise tax "is a clear example of a situation where, if the president had provided the kind of leadership that he could, following the Iranian crisis that began on the fourth of November, he could have called on the American people for some sacrifice in order to relieve our dependence on imported oil" (1/5/80, IA). This is a strong criticism of the sitting president. This statement suggests that Carter failed to provide the needed leadership for our country.

This section examined policy and character forms of utterances. We presented examples of each of the utterance forms with explanations of the trends in the primary debates under review.

TARGET OF ATTACK IN THE 1980 REPUBLICAN DEBATES

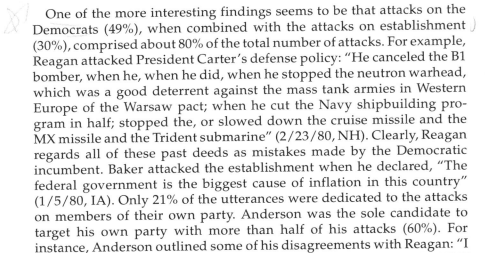

One of the more interesting findings seems to be that attacks on the Democrats (49%), when combined with the attacks on establishment (30%), comprised about 80% of the total number of attacks. For example, Reagan attacked President Carter's defense policy: "He canceled the B1 bomber, when he, when he did, when he stopped the neutron warhead, which was a good deterrent against the mass tank armies in Western Europe of the Warsaw pact; when he cut the Navy shipbuilding program in half; stopped the, or slowed down the cruise missile and the MX missile and the Trident submarine" (2/23/80, NH). Clearly, Reagan regards all of these past deeds as mistakes made by the Democratic incumbent. Baker attacked the establishment when he declared, "The federal government is the biggest cause of inflation in this country" (1/5/80, IA). Only 21% of the utterances were dedicated to the attacks on members of their own party. Anderson was the sole candidate to target his own party with more than half of his attacks (60%). For instance, Anderson outlined some of his disagreements with Reagan: "I do not share his view of the world. He was opposed to the SALT II agreement, even before the invasion of Afghanistan. He was opposed to the Panama Canal treaties" (1/5/80, IA). Clearly, Anderson views these as errors on Reagan's part. See Table 4.4.

Another interesting finding is that the front-runner, Reagan, was attacked the most by all other candidates—24 total attacks from other candidates. The second favorite target of attack was George Bush (16). Bush, Connally, and Reagan were leaders among the candidates in attacking the establishment. Baker was very tough on the Democrats, targeting them with 71% of his attacks. In addition, the only Republican attacked by Reagan was Bush, and Reagan produced the fewest attacks on members of his own party (6%). The bulk of Reagan's attacks were leveled against the Democrats (56%) and the establishment (38%). Thus, these candidates tended to attack the other party more than one another in these debates.

ISSUES ADDRESSED IN THE 1980 REPUBLICAN DEBATES

According to a CBS News/*New York Times* (1980a) public opinion poll, Americans had five major issues that concerned them (taxes/inflation, economy, foreign policy, energy, Iran hostages). However, the largest single group of remarks in these debates can be found in the "other" category (30%). Still, it appears that each candidate addressed just about every single issue. Foreign policy, traditionally a Republican forte, took third place in the public's interest (21%) and was prominent in the discourse of the three debates studied here (25%). The issue that was most salient to the voters—taxes and inflation (23%)—received the most attention from Dole (14), Anderson (12), and Bush (11). See Table 4.5.

TABLE 4.4
Target of Attack in the 1980 Republican Debates

	Own Party (Republicans)								Establishment	Carter/Dems.
	Ander.	Baker	Bush	Conn.	Crane	Dole	Reagan	Other Repub		
Anderson	–	2	1	2	1	1	6	0	5	4
Baker	1	–	3	1	0	0	1	1	0	17
Bush	1	0	–	1	0	0	3	1	16	20
Connally	1	0	5	–	0	0	11	1	18	24
Crane	0	0	0	0	–	0	2	0	2	3
Dole	1	0	1	0	0	–	1	0	1	3
Reagan	0	0	6	0	0	0	–	0	38	57
Total	4	2	16	4	1	1	24	3	80	128
	55 (21%)								(30%)	(49%)

TABLE 4.5
Issues Addressed in the 1980 Republican Debates

	Taxes/ Inflation (23%)	Economy (22%)	Foreign Policy (21%)	Energy (11%)	Iran Hostages (9%)	Other (5%)
Anderson	12	3	10	2	0	11
Baker	5	2	17	9	4	6
Bush	11	5	19	17	4	18
Connally	3	1	15	22	5	14
Crane	6	4	10	2	0	11
Dole	14	3	8	1	0	22
Reagan	5	1	8	9	4	22
Total	56 (16%)	19 (6%)	87 (25%)	62 (18%)	17 (5%)	104 (30%)

CBS News/*New York Times*, 1980a.

DISCUSSION

We will begin by discussing the general functions of the examined discourse. Next we will examine policy versus character forms of utterances. Then discussion will turn to the targets of attacks, and we will offer some possible explanations of the dynamics of these debates. Finally, the issues addressed in the debates and implications will be discussed.

Functions of the 1980 Republican Debates

As stated earlier, the 1980 Republican primary was a relatively positive set of debates. With three-quarters of the utterances dedicated to acclaims, 22% to attacks, and 3% to defenses, it seems clear that candidates focused most of their attention on getting themselves known to the voters and distinguishing their candidacy from that of other contenders. We feel that this approach is reasonable. Early on in the elections process, candidates must make their positions known to the voters and try not to be too negative toward their opponents—after all, everyone wants their party to be elected in the general elections. Of course, the way for candidates to accomplish this goal is to acclaim various aspects of their candidacy before the voters.

Attacks are important instruments of the political discourse, because they can accomplish several goals. First, attacks, if effective, may reduce the capability of the opponent to capture the momentum necessary to secure nomination. An example of this emerged when Reagan, who vowed not to play a divisive role and refused to participate in the debates, began to lose his leading position to Bush. As a result, he was targeted during the debates and later decided to participate. Second, attack may also improve the chances of the candidates by making them appear more thoughtful and concerned with the issues, implying that they would do things differently than their opponents.

In the collection of the examined debates, Connally was the most negative, relying on attacks in 36% of his utterances. He was followed by Reagan (32% attacks) and Anderson (31% attacks). These findings can be explained by the fact that Connally and Anderson had to challenge more favored candidates like Reagan and Bush. A possible explanation of Reagan's negativity is that he saw himself as a clear front-runner and a leader of his party. Interestingly, this suggests that he considered his chief rival to be Carter, because Reagan advanced more attacks against the Democrats than were made by any other Republican candidate by a wide margin. It is also possible that an attack can, at times, function much like an acclaim, because voters could identify with that which a candidate rejects (attacks). That is, when a Republican (like Reagan) attacks a Democrat (like President Carter), the Republican primary voters may consider this attack to represent a desirable (Republican) trait in the candidate.

Topics of the 1980 Republican Debates

As a general trend, this campaign was driven by policy (65% of themes in these debates). Appealing to the voters' dissatisfaction with the policies of the then current Democratic administration, as Reagan did, would increase Reagan's appeal as the presidential candidate. In addition, the whole point of having an election is to choose the candidate who will offer the best program of action for the country; thus focus on the policy aspect of the candidacy may be an especially fruitful approach. This is a utilitarian approach, but it appears to be perfectly reasonable from the benefit-maximizing voter standpoint. Even though policy utterances prevailed in these debates, character utterances made up over a third of the total, so they were another important component of the discourse examined.

An emphasis on acclaiming general goals (42%) appears to be reasonable. General goals are vague, by definition, which allow candidates to talk about policy without presenting anything specific enough to attack. In turn, the public is interested in candidates' positions on policy issues, and this interest can be satisfied by a candidate's asserting statements on general goals.

Discussion of past deeds was also quite common (38%). Past deeds may appear to be "concrete" or "factual" to voters. General goals are common, because they are easy to articulate (and difficult to attack), but we can only speculate on whether future plans will be enacted and

achieve the desired ends. Past deeds, by definition, have already occurred and therefore may appear to be more "true" than other kinds of
policy utterances. Thus, past deeds and general goals may appear to be
better options for candidates than future plans (which accounted for
20% of the policy utterances in these debates).

Among the character utterances, all of the forms (personal qualities,
leadership ability, ideals) overwhelmingly used acclaims over attacks.
This is consistent with the general distribution of the utterances but also
because the public may see character attacks as very personal, thus
increasing the possibility that such attack may backfire. For example,
personal qualities may be perceived as an unreasonable subject of an
attack because it concerns opponents personally. Leadership ability was
the subject that all of the candidates avoided (24%). Attacking ideals,
like general goals, is very difficult; no one wishes to be perceived as
someone saying something like "I do not value freedom."

Target of Attack in the 1980 Republican Debates

One interesting discrepancy between our expectations and findings
concerns the target of attack. It seems likely that during the primaries
candidates (with the possible exception of the front-runner who already
enjoys the lead) have more to gain by attacking one another, thus
reducing the apparent desirability of their opponents. This was not the
case during the 1980 primary debates. Instead, the Democrats were the
most common target of attack in this debates (51% of all attacks). The
fact that attacks on fellow Republicans were less common could have
been due to Reagan's influence: His official reason for abstaining from
the Iowa debate and refusing to criticize other Republicans was the
so-called eleventh commandment. This unwritten rule was eloquently
asserted by Reagan during the Nashua debate in response to an inquiry
about his absence in Iowa:

> Well, what happened—and there are some people here that know this from
> the past and from hearing me. Ever since our party was so factionalized
> and so embittered, dating clear back to the 1964 primaries throughout the
> country—and it was in the 1966 election when I ran for governor in
> California, came up with the eleventh commandment. And we, in just
> those two years later, from that great bitterness, healed the wounds in our
> party. And I've been a missionary preaching unity to the Republican party.
> When I was a Democrat, I used to think that the Republican party was a
> party that would rather win a convention than an election. And so I
> preached it so long, when the whole idea of debate came up, I just thought
> it sounded divisive. It sounded—the idea of Republicans going out again
> in front of the public and airing their differences, and it could lead to
> polarizing the people behind the various candidates, make it more difficult

for them to unify behind whoever might be the winner. Well, I watched the debate, and it didn't create divisiveness. Maybe we've done the job; maybe this party of ours is back together now to where it can afford things of this kind. So I said from then on, "I made a mistake." It was my decision and I said I'll look at them, at the format and if the format appears to be like that one, I will have the confidence that it's not going to be divisive and will accept the invitations to debate. So here I am. (2/23/80, NH)

Overall this passage reflects the spirit of the 1980 Republican primaries. The candidates were oriented more toward electing a candidate from their party than to becoming a front-runner themselves by attacking other candidates.

Nevertheless, an interesting finding was the fact that the front-runner (Reagan) was attacked most frequently of these candidates—24 times. This is reasonable because it supports the idea that candidates have most to gain by tarnishing the candidacy of the front-runner rather than that of other rivals. In other words, an effective attack on the front-runner ought to reduce his or her chances for nomination and increase the chances of other hopefuls.

In addition, although Reagan attacked the least (6%), the only Republican he attacked was Bush. The bulk of Reagan's attacks were leveled against the Democrats (56%) and the establishment (38%). Such a distribution of percentages is not at all surprising. As front-runner, Reagan had little to gain from attacking those candidates who were less popular than him. However, if Reagan was perceived as the leader of his party, he had to pay more attention to challenging the establishment and the opposing party. Furthermore, the one Republican candidate he had the most incentive to attack was Bush, the closest challenger.

Issues Addressed in the 1980 Republican Debates

It is difficult to assess the relationship between the issues candidates discuss in the primary debates and public opinion polls. Certainly voters have concerns they want to be addressed by the candidates, one of whom will be a contestant for the most responsible office in the land. However, the largest group of comments in these debates were devoted to issues other than those that were the five most important to voters in 1980. The issue that was most important to voters (taxes/inflation) received fewer comments that the third issue (foreign policy) or the fourth issue (energy). Only 6% of the candidates' remarks addressed the second most important issue (the economy); 5% of utterances addressed the fifth most important issue (Iran hostages). It does not appear that these candidates focused most of their remarks on the issues that mattered most to voters.

CONCLUSION

This chapter examined three Republican primary debates from 1980. The functions and topics of discourse in these debates were examined along with forms of policy and character utterances, targets of attacks, and issues addressed. Reagan secured the nomination, and despite the fact that Bush characterized Reagan's economic plans as voodoo economics, the Reagan/Bush team defeated Carter/Mondale in 1980.

5

1984 Democratic Primary Debates: Morning Again in America

"Contentious" is one word that might aptly describe the primary season of 1984. Although one team of scholars titled their book on the 1984 election *Wake Us When It's Over: Presidential Politics of 1984* (Germond & Witcover, 1985), and another called the general campaign "vapid and lackluster" (Mansfield, 1987, p. 279), the primary showdown between the Democrats may have been the one part of the show that was worth the price of admission.

It was a campaign of firsts. Jesse Jackson was the first African American to make a serious run for the presidency. The first American to orbit the earth, John Glenn, hoped for a hero's welcome in the campaign, and Walter Mondale, the eventual nominee, would go on to choose the first woman vice presidential candidate for either of the two major parties. So although some might view a campaign against a popular incumbent president as unworthy of study, the primary campaign of 1984 is well worthy of our attention. In this chapter, I will provide a brief background of the primary campaign and debates of 1984 and then move into a more detailed analysis of the debates using the Theory of Political Campaign Discourse.

BACKGROUND OF THE 1984 DEMOCRATIC DEBATES

No fewer than eight prominent Democrats sought the opportunity to run against Ronald Reagan in 1984. All but one had made careers of elected politics, and all had been in public life and service for at least a decade. Despite the fact that he had served as vice president under a losing incumbent president only four years early, Walter Mondale was clearly the first choice of many leaders within the party (Mann, 1985). However, many of the trailing candidates, including eventual finalists Jesse Jackson and Gary Hart, were frustrated with several aspects of the primary process that privileged front-runners such as Mondale. Only two years earlier, the Democratic National Committee's (DNC) Hunt Commission recommended changes in the rules governing the selection of delegates to the national convention, delegates who would choose the eventual nominee (Maisel, 1999; Mann, 1985; Thurow, 1987). In short, the rules enhanced the party leaders' ability to choose the nominee, leaving other candidates largely in the cold. Although Jesse Jackson strongly opposed these proposals in a special meeting with the Democratic National Committee's executive committee in 1982, the proposals were approved, and one of Jackson's main complaints throughout the primary season was the fact that he did not receive a proportion of DNC delegates equal to the proportion of the popular vote he had received (Page, 1990; Wormser, 1984). These rules, and the fact that the primary season had been shortened, gave the front-runner a distinct advantage in the primary race, and early media reports gave Mondale and Glenn the best chances of capturing the nomination (Wormser, 1984).

Walter Mondale enjoyed a great deal of support from the Democratic Party faithful. As vice president under Jimmy Carter, Mondale had been one of the most involved vice presidents in U.S. history. He believed that his weekly discussion breakfasts with the president and his standing invitation to sit in on any meeting open to the president gave him an insight into the presidency that no other candidate could offer (Brookhiser, 1986; Henry, 1985; Wormser, 1984). Mondale was often attacked for his support from organized groups, particularly labor (Brookhiser, 1986; Henry, 1985) but was a longtime supporter of Democratic causes such as civil rights, poverty, and the elderly (Henry, 1985; Wormser, 1984) while a senator from Minnesota. His support of the party even extended to the Vietnam War in its early days, and he called his failure to denounce it sooner his greatest public error (Henry, 1985). Mondale has been described as a cautious candidate, a candidate so supported by his party that his mentor, Hubert Humphrey, once quipped that he was the only man who could be appointed president (Brookhiser, 1986). Ultimately, party support was crucial to Mondale's success (Mann, 1985), but he faced a difficult primary season.

Against the backdrop of an uphill battle against an "heir apparent," seven candidates contested Mondale for the nomination. John Glenn, once an astronaut and then a senator from Ohio, had been touted as a leader very early in the campaign, based on his name recognition and support from key players within the party (Henry, 1985; Wormser,

1984). In fact, early polls demonstrated that when head-to-head against Reagan, Glenn actually out-polled Mondale, a fact that convinced his staff that he actually had a better shot at beating Reagan than Mondale had (Wormser, 1984). His campaign, like his career as a senator, focused primarily on issues of nuclear proliferation and energy. Although Glenn was a hero with the nation's space program, his speaking style was, as several commentators noted, extremely dull (Henry, 1985; Wormser, 1984). Glenn could not generate the support he needed to live up to his hero status and dropped out of the race midway through the primary season.

Another midseason dropout was 1972 Democratic nominee George McGovern, who ran against his former campaign manager, Gary Hart, on a theme of disarmament and antipoverty. McGovern's previous attempt at the presidency in 1972 was doomed when it was revealed that his choice of vice president, Missouri's Thomas Eagleton, had undergone shock treatment therapy for depression in the 1960s (Henry, 1985). After the election, McGovern served one more term in the Senate before his defeat in 1980 (Wormser, 1984). Although no one expected McGovern to win with poor organization and lack of media attention (Henry, 1985), he still hoped to bring his nuclear disarmament message to the fore of public discourse.

Early dropouts in the 1984 primary season included Reuben Askew, the controversial senator and two-term former governor of Florida whose positions on trade and labor issues were exactly the opposite of those embraced by the rest of the Democratic Party; Senate party whip Alan Cranston, who like McGovern focused on issues of nuclear disarmament and was known for his ability to come to pragmatic compromises on key Senate votes; and Ernest Hollings, the South Carolina senator known for his sometimes offensive candor, who suggested an across-the-board freeze on federal spending and called for the Democratic Party to heed less frequently the call of special interest groups (Brookhiser, 1986; Henry, 1985; Wormser, 1984). All of these candidates left the campaign early in the season, so they did not participate in the debates analyzed here.

Mondale's principal opponents in the final days of the campaign, then, were Gary Hart and Jesse Jackson. Hart, a two-time senator from Colorado, was not considered a threat to Mondale early in the campaign. In fact, it seemed for a time that the Hart story most covered by the media was whether or not he would drop out, a charge he spent a great deal of time denying (Henry, 1985). However, his win in New Hampshire made it clear that the senator known as an intellectual idealist who supported a new, more centrist Democratic Party would be a constant competitor throughout the campaign (Mann, 1985). Although he was considered an expert on the stalled SALT (Strategic Arms

Limitations Talks) II treaty, Hart was criticized by Mondale in the debates for failing to come out in support of the nuclear freeze movement in its early days. Hart's campaign was about ideas, particularly those that encouraged national renewal (Wormser, 1984).

Jesse Jackson, Mondale's other competition, represented what many authors (e.g., Collins, 1986; Morris, 1990) considered a potential watershed in U.S. politics. For the first time, an African American was a serious contender for the party's nomination for president, quite an accomplishment for a man who had never held public office. As a past leader of the humanitarian organization Operation PUSH (People United to Save Humanity), Jackson and his campaign continually reached out to the disadvantaged, those he felt had been disenfranchised from the promise of the American dream (Collins, 1986). As the black community embraced him, so did the media (Henry, 1985). Jackson charged that Reagan ignored people in need and promised to champion those who did not have a voice in Reagan's America. He insisted that he did not run a "black" campaign but rather that he hoped to bring all the disenfranchised into a "Rainbow Coalition" that would change the balance of political power (Collins, 1986; Thurow, 1987; Walters, 1990). Despite his idealism and inspirational speaking style, Jackson garnered criticism on a number of fronts. Although he was known for his civil rights activism and connection to Dr. Martin Luther King, other civil rights leaders connected with King described him as egotistical (Wormser, 1984). He also drew fire from the Jewish community for his trip to the Middle East in 1979 in which he publicly embraced PLO (Palestine Liberation Organization) leader Yasser Arafat and criticized U.S. foreign policy toward Israel (Coolidge, 1990), as well as for his well-publicized remarks calling Jewish people "Hymies" and New York "Hymietown" (Thurow, 1987). However, a 1983 trip to Syria, which secured the release of an injured U.S. airman who had been shot down over Lebanon, was a foreign policy success for a man known primarily for his work in domestic affairs (Henry, 1985; Wormser, 1984). Despite what commentators (Collins, 1986; Wormser, 1984) described as weak organization and funding, the enthusiasm Jackson generated within the black community propelled his candidacy to a longer life and broader constituency than many of those candidates with a great deal of experience in elected office (Morris, 1990).

This chapter reports the analysis of three 1984 Democratic primary debates. The first debate, between Glenn, Hart, Jackson, McGovern, and Mondale, was held on March 8, 1984, in Atlanta, Georgia (3/8/84, GA). The second occurred on May 2, 1984, in Grapevine, Texas (5/2/84, TX), and featured Hart, Jackson, and Mondale. The last debate studied here is from June 3, 1984 in Los Angeles, California (6/3/84, CA). It again included Hart, Jackson, and Mondale.

Although all eight candidates participated in at least one primary debate, the debates selected for this sample featured Mondale, Glenn, McGovern, Jackson, and Hart. The three debates cover three distinct periods in the campaign and capture the spirit of both multicandidate debates of the early days of the campaign as well as the more focused debates of the final days of the season. First, we examine the overall functions of the discourse, then analyze the policy and character utterances in the campaign. Next, we take a look at the targets of attacks lodged in the debates, and finally, we briefly examine the candidates' treatment of issues that were considered important by voters.

FUNCTIONS OF THE 1984 DEMOCRATIC DEBATES

In these debates, acclaims accounted for 51% of the candidates' utterances. For example, Gary Hart engaged in an instance of self-praise in the primary debate in Georgia, praising his policy goals and his experience: "I am for reducing the Reagan military buildup by 140 to 150 billions of dollars in the next four to five years. And I've spelled out in great detail as, I think, the only member of this group has ten years of experience on the Arms Services Committee, where those cuts must come" (3/8/84, GA). Like many Democratic voters, Hart opposed the Reagan administration's military spending and thus was able to praise his own plans to reduce that level of spending. Additionally, Hart was also able to contrast his 10 years of experience on the Armed Services Committee with the lack of such experience in the other candidates. By acclaiming both his plans and his experience, Hart made a strong attempt to make himself appear preferable to others in the field. See Table 5.1.

While acclaims are made in an effort to improve a candidate's stature by emphasizing the positive, attacks can make a candidate appear more preferable by emphasizing the ways in which the

TABLE 5.1
Functions of Utterances in the 1984 Democratic Debates

	Acclaims	Attacks	Defenses
Glenn	32 (49%)	30 (46%)	3 (5%)
Hart	73 (43%)	84 (49%)	14 (8%)
Jackson	105 (50%)	97 (46%)	7 (4%)
McGovern	16 (48%)	17 (52%)	0
Mondale	123 (58%)	71 (34%)	17 (8%)
Total	349 (51%)	299 (43%)	41 (6%)

competition appears substantially less preferable. Attacks comprised 43% of the statements in these debates. For instance, in the same Georgia debate where Hart had emphasized his experience with military issues, John Glenn lodged an attack against his position and experience on the exact same issues: "Gary mentioned the [aircraft] carriers. He and I had a debate which I'm sure he'll recall on the Senate floor about two years ago on that. He talks about the cheaper carrier as the smaller one. But it shows such a lack of fundamental understanding of how sea power works because you have to have a whole task force that goes with any carrier that gets out there" (3/8/84, GA). In this instance, Glenn demonstrated that Hart did not fully understand the kind of deployment that must take place when a smaller carrier is used instead of a larger one. In making this statement, Glenn hoped to make himself look more preferable than Hart by making Hart look less knowledgeable and experienced. Such an attack enhanced Glenn's stature at the expense of Hart's.

Finally, in response to attacks, candidates will sometimes offer defenses. Six percent of comments in these debates were defenses. In the California primary debate, it was suggested that Hart has "danced right up to the call for an investigation" into allegations of unethical activity with regard to Mondale's support among unaffiliated super-delegates to the Democratic National Convention. Hart responded to this attack with this defense: "No, Mr. Brokaw, I haven't danced up to anything. What we did was file a complaint with the Federal Election Commission, questioning the legality of the five hundred thousand to a million dollars of political action committee funds which Mr. Mondale said that he was going to give back and hasn't" (6/3/84, CA). When Brokaw accused Hart of practically calling for an investigation into Mondale's activities, Hart defended himself from the attack by providing a flat denial of that claim. In doing so, he hoped to minimize or rise above any negative perceptions the attack might have caused in the minds of voters.

TOPICS OF THE 1984 DEMOCRATIC DEBATES

A popular assertion concerning political campaigns is that they emphasize candidate image at the expense of substantive discussion (e.g., Center for Responsive Politics, 1988). This assertion was tested within this chapter, because the Functional Theory of Political Campaign Discourse analyzes topics of political utterances in two main categories, policy and character. After an utterance is coded into the policy or character category, it is also coded into one of the three subcategories of policy or character. The 1984 primary debates were coded into one of two main categories, as well as into one of the six subcategories, and this section explores the results of that analysis in greater detail, with explanations and examples of each of the forms.

In these 1984 primary debates, over twice as many themes addressed policy (70%) as character (30%; see Table 5.2). Walter Mondale addressed his policy preferences concerning the United States' relationship with the Soviet Union during the Atlanta debate, explaining: "I agree that the idea of just building up arms to sort of scare the Russians so that then they will agree to whatever we want, as Reagan has demonstrated, will fail. I want to be understood as totally committed to annual summit conferences, to arms control negotiations, to efforts to reduce tensions" (3/8/84, GA). Clearly, Mondale focused on a theme dealing with America's foreign policy toward the Soviet Union. Likewise, Jackson was asked about his views on policy toward the Middle East, and he chose to criticize U.S. policies that focused on Israel to the exclusion of other actors in that region: "If you keep talking with Israel only, and don't stop Israel's enemies from being her enemies, you cannot help Israel" (6/3/84, CA). Both candidates, then, dealt with policy issues in these statements.

However, character did not go unrepresented in these debates. In Georgia, Hart acclaimed a personal quality: "I was only one of about 15 senators that had the courage to support this administration" (3/8/84, GA). Jackson emphasized two qualities that are important to a leader: "That means having leadership that's bold enough and courageous enough to meet with all forces" (6/3/84, CA). So both policy and character discussions figured prominently in the 1984 primary debates.

Statements of policy fall into one of three categories: past deeds, future plans, and general goals. Utterances concerning past deeds deal with what a candidate has done (or perhaps has failed to do) in policy areas, particularly when the candidate has a record in public office. Candidates often spend time acclaiming their own past deeds,

TABLE 5.2
Policy vs. Character in the 1984 Democratic Debates

	Policy	Character
Glenn	45 (73%)	17 (27%)
Hart	107 (68%)	50 (32%)
Jackson	153 (76%)	49 (24%)
McGovern	24 (73%)	9 (27%)
Mondale	126 (65%)	68 (35%)
Total	455 (70%)	193 (30%)

TABLE 5.3
Forms of Policy and Character in the 1984 Democratic Debates

	Policy						Character					
	Past Deeds*		Future Plans		General Goals		Personal Qualities		Leadership Ability		Ideals	
Glenn	10	21	3	4	3	4	0	0	6	1	10	0
Hart	9	49	7	5	31	6	3	18	6	5	17	1
Jackson	10	58	1	10	66	8	1	16	6	4	21	1
McGovern	0	13	1	0	6	4	0	0	1	0	8	0
Mondale	8	45	9	4	55	5	13	13	16	2	22	2
Total	37	186	21	23	161	27	17	47	35	12	78	4
	223 (49%)		44 (10%)		188 (40%)		64 (33%)		47 (24%)		82 (43%)	

but they can be attacked for past deeds as well. In this debate, past deeds accounted for almost half (49%) of all policy utterances (see Table 5.3). An example of such an attack occurred when Glenn attacked Hart's record on defense: "Mr. Hart opposed the F-15, the F-18, and the B-1 . . . the Nimitz carrier, the Minuteman III, the AWACs add-on, the Patriot Hellfire MLRS missiles, and has gone to a program of leadership in Washington of smaller and simpler is better, rather than stressing our technology, and that's a fundamental difference between us" (3/8/84, GA). Although voters may not have known much about the alphabet soup of national defense Glenn described, they will clearly understand that Glenn is suggesting that Hart's past opposition of such projects makes him unfit to command the military now. Glenn once again hoped that his past record on these issues appeared superior to Hart's.

A candidate's future plans may also be an important area of discussion. Future plans are specific proposals for change (means) that have been advanced or supported by the candidate. These candidates devoted 10% of their policy comments to discussion of future plans. In the Texas debate, Mondale explained his position on specific issues related to defense: "In many ways I have stood for a strong defense, and I stand for a strong defense. I just want to give one example. The B-1, which I oppose, I support the Stealth because it's a modern, advanced bomber that will take us into the next century. . . . I am against the MX, but I am for the Minuteman" (3/8/84, Ga). In this instance, Mondale tells his audience unequivocally which weapons systems he would continue and which weapons systems he would likely discontinue. By presenting his plans for the future, he hoped to gain support among those who believed that certain defense programs should be cut. In the California debate, Hart attacked Mondale's future plans when he questioned Mondale's support of the domestic content bill, a trade initiative that required foreign manufacturers to meet a threshold percentage of U.S.-made parts and labor in a vehicle before it could be sold in the United States: "The domestic content bill, a major difference in this campaign, is economic surrender. It says, we cannot operate and maintain efficient automobile plants. We'll trade a few jobs here; it'll cost us ten jobs for every one we save" (6/3/84, CA). Mondale's plans for the future included support for the domestic content bill, and Hart asserted that it would do far more harm than good. In making this argument, Hart hoped to show Mondale's plans for the future were not good for the country, making Mondale a less attractive choice for the presidency.

A final policy category, less specific than future plans, is a candidate's general goals. General goals deal primarily with general directions or positions on issues, where a candidate does not present or endorse a specific policy option. General goals constituted 40% of the policy remarks in these debates. In the Texas debate, Jesse Jackson addressed illegal immigration by presenting a series of general goals: "Unless we deal with crippling poverty and disease across the border that people are fleeing from, and sometimes the tyranny, if you went into that banana republic. We are dealing with the symptoms, the end result. The causal factors are a hemisphere issue that our government must address. After all, these are our neighbors" (5/2/84, TX). Rather than endorsing a particular policy or presenting a new policy of his own, Jackson hopes to show that the United States' entire approach to the problem of illegal immigration is ineffective. His argument here, that the direction of the policy should be changed, does not suggest what countries the government should deal with, or how disease could be eliminated, but rather presents an idea he hopes voters will appreciate.

Candidate statements can also be coded as character utterances, which fall into one of three categories: personal qualities, leadership ability, or ideals. Personal qualities focus on the candidate's values and ethics and may include such issues as conduct of personal life, personal integrity, and campaign ethics. One third of comments (33%) in these debates addressed personal qualities. Such an attack was levied against Mondale by Hart in the California debate:

There's an ad, I understand, Mr. Mondale says he hasn't seen his ads, his television ads, I can tell him about one that's running in New Jersey now. It has a pistol—we differ over what kind of national gun control, laws there ought to be—Mr. Mondale, because of that difference, has pistol which rotates toward the viewer, the chamber turns, and the barrel ends up pointed right at the viewer, and strongly suggests that I would needlessly endanger people's safety or their lives. He knows that's not the truth. (6/3/84, CA)

With this statement, Hart attacks Mondale's personal qualities on two fronts. First, Hart points out that Mondale says he's never seen any of his television ads, which does seem a little farfetched for a candidate in the middle of the most important campaign of his career. Thus, Hart suggests perhaps Mondale is not being completely honest. Second, relying on the assumption that Mondale did indeed know about the ads, Hart insists that Mondale is lying—that he knows Hart would not support dangerous legislation. Both arguments are aimed at exposing Mondale's undesirable personal qualities.

Another possible area of discussion concerning character is a candidate's leadership ability, which might include utterances where candidates discuss past governmental posts or experience in dealing with international leaders or perhaps even experience leading a nation-wide business or nonprofit organization. Leadership comments accounted for one-quarter (24%) of character remarks. As the only candidate with experience in the executive branch of the federal government, Mondale hoped to stress his unique experience as a true participant in the activities of the Carter administration, particularly the task of choosing a cabinet: "One of the things I think I would bring in terms of a strength to the presidency is that I have been there. I know how a cabinet works, I know how important it is to pick them so they can work together. I know about the sub-cabinet and the rest, and I think a cabinet has to be picked with great care. . . . And the time has to be taken by someone who knows what he's doing, so it's done properly" (6/3/84, CA). Of course, Mondale is very explicit in emphasizing his leadership abilities in this particular statement, reminding the audience that he was the only candidate with an intimate knowledge of the responsibilities of the presidency.

A final area of discussion concerning character focuses on candidates' ideals, which tend to focus on such revered notions as individual rights, freedoms, and opportunities. Ideals comprised 43% of the character utterances in these debates. In discussing the legacy of the New Deal–era government and the role of a modern president, Mondale pointed out: "Finally, we need a president who leads us toward justice. And I mean enforcing those Civil Rights Acts. I mean ratifying that Equal Rights Amendment. I mean standing up for the social security and Medicare. This country must be fair, and the history of America is that when a president leads us toward fairness and toward our future it can be done" (3/8/84, GA). Here Mondale sandwiches acclaims of his general goals between statements that share his vision for the country and his emphasis on an important value, justice. By pointing to ideals that are common to most U.S. voters, Mondale hoped to gain their support at the polls.

TARGET OF ATTACK IN THE 1984 DEMOCRATIC DEBATES

Primary campaigns involve candidates from the same party, candidates who obviously share many of the same ideals, philosophies, and approaches. Many primary candidates have served together in the House or Senate and have known one another for entire careers. Such circumstances might suggest that primary campaigns are amiable affairs between friends. However, it seems that the relative similarity between many primary candidates makes it even more important that candidates make efforts to emphasize their differences for the voters' benefit. Rather than a friendly encounter, primary campaigns can be very difficult for the candidates and the party, as Trent and Friedenberg (2000) observe: "Many professional politicians and party leaders hate the primary stage of a campaign because a genuine primary is a fight within the family of the party—a fight that can turn nasty as different factions within the family compete with each other to secure a place on the November ballot for their candidate" (p. 33). Keeping in mind that the candidates must defeat one another before they are able to turn their focus to the other party, it seems appropriate that candidates would attack one another more than the other party, that candidates would attack the front-runner more than other candidates, and that front-runners might want to maintain an "above the battle" posture by focusing on the other party. The Functional Theory provides an opportunity to test these assertions, and this section discusses how these hypotheses faired in the 1984 primary debates.

First, the candidates in the 1984 primary debates tended to attack the other party, particularly Ronald Reagan, more than they attacked each other. Table 5.4 reveals that Democrats involved in these three primary debates attacked one another 126 times, for 42% of the total attacks, whereas they attacked the other party (which includes the Reagan administration) 146 times, for 49% of the total. Jackson, for example, attacked Reagan's tax policy in the Texas debate: "Under Mr. Reagan, there were 95 corporations that made a profit last year and paid no taxes. And that is a rip-off. Under his arrangement, the rich are taking from the poor—a kind of reverse Robin Hood process" (5/2/84, TX). Here Jackson attacks the policies of the administration, rather than his opponents in this particular race. Mondale engages in the same sort of attack, focusing on the administration's defense policy: "[Mr. Reagan]

TABLE 5.4
Target of Attack in the 1984 Democratic Debates

	Democrats						Establish- ment	Repub.
	Glenn	Hart	Jackson	McGovern	Mondale	Own Party		
Glenn	—	13	0	0	5	0	1	10
Hart	3	–	6	1	27	1	11	35
Jackson	0	15	–	0	14	9	10	50
McGovern	1	0	2	–	1	0	2	11
Mondale	0	21	0	0	–	7	3	40
Total	4	49	8	1	47	17	27	146
	(3%)	(39%)	(6%)	(1%)	(37%)	(13%)	(9%)	(49%)
	126 (42%)							

would have the American people believe that we're [militarily] stronger. In fact, there is a lot of evidence that through his management of foreign policy, through the use of money that actually, in a way, has actually reduced preparedness and readiness of our armed forces. We are not stronger; we are weaker" (5/2/84, TX). Mondale's attack focuses on the past deeds of the administration, rather than attempting to differentiate himself from his primary opponents. Attacks on the other party, then, were popular strategies in these primary debates.

However, when candidates did attack one another, they tended to target the front-runners—Hart and Mondale—more frequently than other candidates. Hart and Mondale were attacked at virtually the same level, with 39% of the attacks launched against Hart and 37% of the attacks in the debates against Mondale. The next closest Democratic target, Jackson, received a mere 6% of the total attacks. Jackson, for example, attacked both Hart and Mondale for their reluctance to choose a woman for a running mate: "If Mr. Hart and Mondale would not share that ticket with a woman, while women are 50% of our convention, they then add to the misery of women who need to become empowered" (3/8/84, GA). Here Jackson attempts to position himself more favorably by demonstrating that the front-runners are unwilling to accommodate a key Democratic constituency.

While it has been suggested that front-runners may focus their own attacks toward the other party in anticipation of the general election battle, this was not the case in the 1984 primaries. It does not appear that front-runner status caused Mondale or Hart to attack the Reagan administration any more than their primary opponents did. Although Mondale, who was a leader throughout the campaign, spent 56% of his attacks on the Republican Party, his sometime co-front-runner Hart focused more attacks (45%) on fellow Democrats than on the Republican Party (42%). Jackson and McGovern, however, tallied high percentages of attacks on Republicans (51% and 65%, respectively), whereas Glenn focused more of his attacks on his own party (62%). Criticism of the advantages Mondale gained through the change in the delegate rules led him to go on the offensive in the California debate, attacking both Jackson and Hart: "Their essential position is something like this: I know, Mondale, that you won New York, but I'd like to have your delegates anyway. I know you won Pennsylvania and Illinois and so on, and I believe I'm going to win California, and New Jersey, and some of the other states on Tuesday, but we'd like your delegates" (6/3/84, CA). Here, Mondale suggests that Hart and Jackson were unfair to argue that the delegates should be allocated differently. In making these attacks against members of his own party, he is doing the typical business of a primary campaign—separating himself from the other candidates from his party.

Attacks on the status quo, or the establishment, were far less prominent in these primary debates, comprising merely 27 (9%) of the total attacks. Jackson, the only candidate without Washington experience, and Hart, whose ideas were sometimes perceived as outside the party's lines, lodged the most attacks against the standard operating procedures of Washington. Hart, in his criticism of Mondale's support for the domestic content bill, levied attacks against the status quo's handling of trade policies and domestic production, arguing, "We need to modernize. We didn't do it in the seventies, we're not doing it in the eighties. We need to become productive" (6/3/84, CA). His criticism extends beyond the Reagan administration to include Presidents Carter, Ford, and Nixon, as well as other members of government who did not make efforts to improve the United States' manufacturing base. Such an attack is less focused and is utilized less in these primary debates. In the 1984 primary debates, then, the opposing party seemed to bear the brunt of most of the attacks, whereas the front-runners handled their own share of attacks from within the party. Attacks against the status quo, however, were minimal.

ISSUES ADDRESSED IN THE 1984 DEMOCRATIC DEBATES

One final aspect of the 1984 primary debates that was analyzed for this study involved the candidates' adherence to topics of importance for voters. In these debates, the candidates spent the majority of their utterances discussing issues of importance to voters (65%) (see Table 5.5). The most important issue to voters was the economy, which was addressed by 9% of the policy utterances in these debates. In California, for example, Jackson talked about his goals for economic improvement:

TABLE 5.5
Issues Addressed in the 1984 Democratic Debates

	Economy (18%)	Jobs (14%)	War (11%)	Other Domestic (10%)	Budget Deficit (8%)	Other (39%)
Glenn	6	4	15	7	2	13
Hart	7	7	34	30	2	63
Jackson	20	8	42	48	5	69
McGovern	9	1	13	20	1	5
Mondale	11	3	44	36	7	62
Total	53 (9%)	23 (4%)	148 (25%)	141 (24%)	17 (3%)	212 (36%)

CBS/*New York Times*, 1984.

"I need your support to redirect the course of our nation from a wartime economy to a peacetime economy" (6/3/84, CA). The second most important issue was jobs or unemployment, which was the topic of 4% of the comments in these debates. In Georgia, for instance, Mondale attacked Hart's proposed $10 per barrel tax on oil: "[A] half a million people lose their jobs" (3/8/84, GA). War and nuclear war, cited as the third most important issue to voters, received 25% of the utterances in these debates (second only to the themes in the "other" category). In Texas, Jackson addressed this topic, declaring, "I happen to be convinced that we are in a position now that there is no defense against a nuclear attack upon us by the Russians. Or vice versa. We have the capacity to wipe each other out. We are beyond defense now. Simply into terror. We must have an aggressive move now to disarm this world" (5/2/84, TX). The deficit was the fifth most important topic and accounted for a mere 1% of the candidates' remarks. For example, Mondale discussed the deficit as he attacked the incumbent Republican administration: "These enormous deficits of 200 billion dollars a year as far as the eye can see, guarantee that long term, sustainable healthy economic growth is impossible, and we're loading our kids with a trillion dollar bill that they've got to repay with interest. It's the worst deliberate, major economic mistake of modern times" (3/8/84, GA).

Thus, these excerpts illustrate how the candidates addressed these topics in the debates analyzed here. Although candidates did tend to address issues of importance to voters, the most important issues did not receive the most attention.

DISCUSSION

As noted above, a number of interesting results arise from this analysis of the 1984 presidential primary debates. In this discussion, the functions will be discussed first, followed by the topics, target of attack, and issues addressed.

Functions of the 1984 Democratic Debates

The comparative nature of political contests makes it imperative for candidates to make themselves appear preferable to their opponents. Such was the case in this series of primary debates. Acclaims outnumbered attacks by over 8% (51% to 43%), with defenses in a distant third place (6%). The relative proportions of these three functions reflect the delicate balance candidates must maintain in a campaign. In this balance, candidates must remain mostly positive to satisfy voters, who profess to dislike mudslinging, while at the same time levying a sufficient number of attacks so that their opponents' weaknesses do not go unchallenged. In these primary debates, this balance seemed to be maintained.

Topics of the 1984 Democratic Debates

In the 1984 primary debates, policy utterances clearly took the lead over character issues (70% to 30%), demonstrating that these debates did indeed promote discussion of substantive issues. Indeed, this same finding holds true across many message forms, as Benoit and his associates found when studying presidential debates (Benoit, Blaney, & Pier, 1998; Benoit & Brazeal, in press; Benoit & Harthcock, 1999b), keynote addresses (Benoit, Blaney, & Pier, 2000), television spots (Benoit, 1999), and acceptance addresses (Benoit, Wells, Pier, & Blaney, 1999). Generally, then, this study lends support for the notion that political campaigns have a tendency to focus on policy more than character.

Looking beyond the overall finding that policy discussion occurred more frequently than character discussion, one of the most important features of the 1984 primary debates was their focus on two policy forms, past deeds and general goals. Between them, these two forms of policy utterance comprised almost 90% of the total utterances. Moreover, the functions of these two policy forms were very different—the vast majority of the past deeds utterances were attacks (83%), whereas the vast majority of the general goals utterances were acclaims (86%). Attacking past deeds is not a surprising strategy, given the amount of experience in the Democratic field and in the opposing party. In the field of Democrats, each candidate had long careers full of past deeds that were open to criticism from opponents—Mondale had served as vice president; Cranston, Hart, Hollings, and Glenn were experienced senators, as was McGovern, who had run for president in 1972; and Askew had experience as a governor; only Jesse Jackson had not held elected office. Of course, the past deeds of the Reagan administration were also frequently attacked in these exchanges. Candidates with so much experience have a record that can be analyzed and attacked by others, and attacks on past deeds are particularly effective because they involve what has already been done and documented. Candidates cannot change the past and often they cannot ignore it; thus, they must find a way to explain their past deeds in a manner that is acceptable to the voters. When candidates engage in such defenses, they are taken off message, appear defensive, and often need to repeat the attacks in order to respond to them. Thus, past deeds were discussed often because they are often fruitful ground for attacking opponents.

Conversely, general goals were discussed so frequently in these debates because they are fertile ground for acclaims. Just as attacks are necessary to bring opponents' undesirable qualities to light, acclaims are necessary to show the positives of each candidate, and candidates in these debates focused far more of their acclaims on general goals than on any other type of acclaim. It might seem counterintuitive for candidates to avoid acclaiming their future plans, given that voters want to know what to expect in the future. However, there is a distinct advantage to stressing general goals over future plans. While a general goal is a rather vague discussion of a broad direction a candidate might take on a particular policy, a future plan is much more fixed and concrete—and much more vulnerable to attack. Specific plans provide specific points of possible attack, and attacking a specific policy is much easier than attacking a general goal, which is inherently more vague. During an interesting exchange in the Texas debate concerning Mondale's views on defense, Hart shows insight into the strategic advantages of stressing general goals over future plans: "What I have tried to do in this presidential debate is elevate the dialogue away from the conventional rhetoric about, well, I'm for a strong defense. Well, who is for weak defense? I don't think you're gonna find anybody who is for weak defense. The question is how to allocate the usable dollars in the most effective ways" (5/2/84, TX). Hart's comment revealed his frustration with discussions that focus on policy but do not achieve the depth he desired. In spite of Hart's desire to discuss more intricate details of public policy, this analysis shows he was unsuccessful in shifting debate away from general goals to future plans. Candidates see the benefits of giving opponents, scholars, and the media as little time as possible to attack their future plans. Although it may not have been the case here, a candidate whose plans are attacked by other candidates and the media may appear to be less capable of crafting policy when compared to candidates who haven't taken the chance of articulating one, and thus many candidates will not take a chance on presenting specific policy options.

In these primary debates, it is clear that policy discussions far outweighed character discussions, with the bulk of the conversation focusing on past deeds and general goals. Additionally, these debates illustrate the strategic advantages of attacking opponents' past deeds while acclaiming one's own general plans.

As noted earlier, character issues took a backseat to policy issues in these primary debates. However, when candidates spent time discussing character issues, they spent more of their time discussing ideals than any other form of character. It is not surprising that candidates would choose to devote time to sharing their ideals, One might even call these statements the rhetorical equivalent of waving flags and kissing babies. Rarely are candidates attacked for their ideals because they are so widely appreciated by voters and, like general goals, are so vague that they do not give opponents much ground to attack. In these debates, candidates shared their own ideals 78 times, while attacking the ideals of others only 4 times, demonstrating that ideals are popular sources for character acclaims.

Target of Attack in the 1984 Democratic Debates

Several issues were explored in relationship to the target of attack in the 1984 primary debates. First of all, although primary debaters at times focus their attacks on opponents from their own party in an effort to win the nomination, in these primary debates the candidates actually attacked the other party more than their own (49% to 42%). One cause for this anomaly may actually be Reagan himself. Scholars of party in government (e.g., Stone, Rapoport, & Abramowitz, 1994; Wattenberg, 1986) contend that Reagan was a force that energized cohesion in both the Republican and Democratic Parties. For the Republican Party, Reagan gave a simple, clear, feel-good message that inspired many of them to mobilize in favor of the party. On the other hand, Reagan's hard-line ideological positions were so galling to the Democrats that they were inspired to mobilize against him. In fact, Wattenberg (1986) observes that "since the onset of academic survey research, no victorious presidential candidate has ever been more intensely disliked among his opponents" (p. 221). In these debates, then, it may well be that each of the candidates found Reagan's policies and positions so completely counter to their personal convictions that they could not help but talk about him. For example, Hart made numerous attacks on Ronald Reagan in the California debate:

> This president has turned his back on equal rights for women; he has not cleaned up one of the toxic waste dumps that plague a very progressive state, New Jersey. He has not ended the arms race, he has accelerated the

nuclear arms race, and as the parent of an eighteen year old son, he scares me to death in terms of my son's safety in Central America, the Persian Gulf, or elsewhere. Those are the issues: a runaway nuclear arms race, a two hundred billion dollar annual deficit that is a mortgage against my children's future, runaway pollution, selling off our environment to the highest bidder, turning his back on equal rights and civil rights. There is so much to run against this president on, I can't wait. (6/3/84, CA)

In a short space of time, then, Hart has referred to a number of problems with the Reagan administration's handling of the country's affairs. His eagerness to attack Reagan is clear. Indeed, this may have been the sentiment of all the Democratic candidates, who clearly found it more interesting to attack the past deeds of the opposing party than to attack the past deeds of each other.

A second interesting finding for the 1984 primary debates deals with the front-runner as a target of attack. It seems intuitive that the party's front-runner has been the target of more attacks than his opponents. After all, it does not make sense for trailing candidates to bring down other trailing candidates and leave the front-runner untouched. Interestingly, in this race, there were actually two front-runners. Mondale was the candidate favored by the party elite and led the pack in the early polls (Mann, 1985), but Hart mounted a serious challenge to Mondale's candidacy early in the primary season. Despite the fact that he was not highly visible or well funded early in the campaign, Hart was able to take New Hampshire and several of the caucuses and primaries immediately after (Davis, 1997; Mann, 1985; Wormser, 1984). This was the beginning of what Mann called a "long and often bitter battle" with Hart (and later Jackson, who drew upon the African-American voters that had been a key Mondale constituency). Thus, for a time Hart was also a front-runner, and both he and Mondale were subject to most of the attacks from their opponents (39% and 37% of same-party attacks, respectively). As a consequence, Hart and Mondale are also responsible for nearly all of the defenses in these primary debates (31 of 41). Thus, it appears that the front-runner in these debates was indeed the prime target of attack within the party.

It has also been suggested that when front-runners attack, they actually look ahead to the opponents in the general election in an effort to appear presidential and above the fray. In this case, then, it would seem plausible that the front-runner would attack the other party more than the other candidates did, whereas the other candidates would attack their own party more than the front-runners did. In these primary debates, however, neither was the case. While it is true that the clear front-runner, Mondale, did attack the Republicans more than most of the other candidates did (56% to 39%), the other front-runner, Hart, attacked his Democratic opponents more than the Republicans (45% to 42%). In addition, two non-front-runners, Jackson and McGovern, devoted similar or even higher percentages of their attacks to the Republicans than Mondale did (51% and 65%, respectively). Once again, this eagerness to attack the other party may be due, in part, to Ronald Reagan. At the same time that the front-runner was not the clear leader in attacks on the other party, it is also true that it is not completely clear that the other candidates were more interested in attacking within the party than the front-runners. While Mondale devoted a mere 39% of his attacks to his own party, and the other front-runner, Hart, devoted 45% of his attacks to his own party, Jackson and McGovern devoted 39% and 24% of their utterances, respectively, to their own party. Only Glenn, who devoted 62% of his attacks to his own party, seemed to clearly be more interested in attacking his own party than the Republicans. Thus, the contention that front-runners would attack the other party more than other candidates did is not borne out by the findings here.

The main target of attack in the 1984 primary debates, then, was the Republican Party, rather than the opponents within the Democratic party. Front-runners did not seem to devote more attacks to the other party than non-front-runners, and the trailing candidates did not focus more of their attacks on the Democratic candidates than the front-runners did. It seems that the Reagan administration was the main target of attacks in these debates.

Issues Addressed in the 1984 Democratic Debates

As noted above, the candidates devoted most of their comments to issues of importance to voters (64% to 36%). However, the distribution of candidate topics did not mirror the rank order of these topics to voters.

The disparity in the topics discussed and the topics of importance may owe to several factors. First of all, the candidates may not have been aware of or interested in discussing what the voters were most interested in hearing. Additionally, the candidates' own areas of expertise may have influenced the topics they chose to highlight. Hart, Glenn, and McGovern all had a great deal of interest and experience in issues related to war, peace, and the military. Mondale had been vice president under a president who was very active in foreign policy, and Jackson had made several trips abroad to meet with foreign leaders prior to his run for the presidency. Each of the candidates spent time in the debates discussing their views on foreign policy at great length, and this may contribute to the disproportionate emphasis of utterances on war and nuclear war. A final reason for the disparity between voter preference and candidate utterance may be the questions posed by the moderators.

Moderators may have chosen questions that were most interesting to them, that seemed to cover the most controversial issues, or that they felt were the key issues of the campaign. All of these factors may have contributed to the focus on issues of war and nuclear war in these primary debates.

CONCLUSION

Three primary debates from the 1984 election cycle were examined utilizing the Functional Theory of Political Campaign Discourse. Acclaims outnumbered both attacks and defenses, and discussion of policy issues outstripped character discussion. Interestingly, front runners did not attack the opposing party more than other Democratic candidates. Indeed, nearly all the Democratic candidates seemed more interested in attacking the Reagan administration than one another, and while the candidates did focus more on issues of importance to voters than on other issues, the most important issues did not receive the most attention.

1988 Primary Debates: What After Reagan?

The 1988 presidential campaign provides another opportunity to study the Functional Theory of Political Campaign Discourse in presidential primary debates. The 1987–1988 primary season is an important one for the study of campaign discourse. There was an unprecedented increase in the number of joint appearances by candidates during that primary season. The candidates engaged in approximately 70 joint appearances during the 1988 campaign (Royer, 1994). These joint appearances often took the form of quasi-debates. Best and Hubbard (2000) indicated that the number of events officially billed as debates increased from 11 in 1984 to 21 in 1988.

Little academic attention has been directed toward the 1988 presidential primary debates. Kendall (2000) occasionally referred to the 1988 primary debates in her in-depth analysis of 20-year cycles in presidential primaries. Davis (1997) briefly discussed the Republican and Democratic primary debates, arguing that DuPont might have helped Bush in a debate in New Hampshire when Dole declined to sign a no-new-tax pledge advocated by DuPont. Davis also repeated the characterization of the Democratic candidates as the seven dwarfs, offered by some press corps members. Jackson was judged by Davis and others as the most able debater, although Jackson was not able to "overcome his limitations as a left-of-center challenger in a party looking for a moderate, middle-of-the-road nominee" (Davis, 1997, p. 152). Davis concluded that so many debates by the Democratic candidates did not catch the public's attention and that the candidates appeared stale and rehearsed by the end of the primary debates. Perhaps the number of primary debates had reached a point of maximum utility.

Lenart (1994) studied the effects of the 1987–1988 primary debates on voters. He found that it was more difficult for voters to judge debate performances when there were three or more candidates rather than two candidates. This second situation, debates involving only two debaters, is the more common situation in the general election race (the only general debates with three candidates occurred in 1992, with Bush, Clinton, and Perot). The large number of candidates that often participate in primary debates may be an inherent liability during the part of the campaign that winnows a potentially large group of contenders down to two nominees (of the major political parties).

Although the 1988 primary debates have been the topic of some research, clearly additional study of the democratic dialogue in these debates is warranted. This chapter will feature the results of a functional analysis of the debate discourse in one Republican and two Democratic debates from the 1987–88 primary season.

BACKGROUND OF THE 1988 PRIMARY DEBATES

Explication of historical context can be valuable to understand the larger discourse as it relates to these debates (Murphy, 1992). Between 1984 and 1987, the Reagan-Bush administration had come under fire in several substantive areas. The Iran-Contra scandal brought to the attention of both Congress and the public after November 1986 that the administration was engaged in secret foreign policy activities designed to circumvent the expressed will of the Congress in foreign affairs. When it became apparent that higher-level officials in the administration had in fact coordinated the actions of lower-level employees, such as Colonel Oliver North, the image of the Reagan-Bush administration was tarnished. The economy was less prosperous toward the end of 1987, certainly less rosy than it had appeared in the 1984 election. In November 1987, for example, the stock market experienced the most significant single-day drop in its history (Brinkley, 1995). In addition, growing numbers of buyouts and takeovers, as well as insider trading scandals, contributed to doubts about the nation's economy. This gives some indication of the situation facing both Republican and Democratic candidates for their party's nomination.

Interestingly, the winners of both the Republican (Dole) and the Democratic (Harkin) caucuses in Iowa failed to ultimately gain the nomination. This made it more difficult for any candidate to secure the nomination early in the primary season and likely contributed to the contentious character and high number of debates.

Quasi-debate appearances commenced very early in the 1987–1988 presidential primary season. A year before the Democratic National convention the first Democratic debate was featured on *Firing Line* on CNN (Davis, 1997). A week later, Republican candidates appeared under the same auspices.

In this chapter, we will analyze three debates, one between Republican primary candidates and two between Democrats. The Republican debate was held in Houston, Texas, on October 28, 1987 and featured on the television program *Firing Line*. The first Democratic debate occurred at the Iowa State Fair in Des Moines on August 23, 1987. The second was also held in Des Moines on January 15, 1988.

THE REPUBLICANS

Several Republican candidates joined in the October 28, 1987, debate in Texas: George Bush, Bob Dole, Pete DuPont, Alexander Haig, Jack Kemp, and Pat Robertson. Bush and Dole enjoyed the advantage of name recognition when compared to the other candidates (Kendall, 2000).

Functions of the 1987 Republican Debate

As in most other primary debates, acclaims predominated in this primary debate. In this debate, acclaims (73%) were more prevalent than attacks (26%), which were in turn more frequent than defenses (1%). For instance, Pat Robertson acclaimed his previous experience: "You may have seen me on the 700 Club television show. What you may not realize is that I'm also in charge of a major United States Cable Network that has 37 million households in all 50 states. Plus I was privileged to found a graduate level university, five graduate schools and a law school" (10/28/87, TX). In a contrasting instance, DuPont attacked the leadership abilities of George Bush: "But the question is in a Bush presidency, where would he lead America? So far we haven't seen any vision, any principles, any policy, we really haven't had it spelled out successfully" (10/28/87, TX). DuPont then launched into an attack on Bush's ambiguous policy position on the INF (Intermediate-Range Nuclear Forces) Treaty: "In our campaign, the INF treaty is a good example of that; we're waiting for details and we're hearing generalities, and I think the question, I think the question is we ought to hear some specifics" (10/28/87, TX). Bush then defended against attacks on his support for the INF Treaty:

> On the question of the INF treaty, I told you all these European leaders are for it. I'm for it, the President's for it, the Joint Chiefs are for it, and I don't see why you can't say hey if its verifiable it's a good idea to get rid of 1600 warheads from the Soviet Union for 400 of ours and then go on and do

what I've said and work on conventional forces, work on chemical weapons. I put the treaty on the table in Geneva to ban chemical weapons. It's
fine when you're outside carping, and criticizing a President, criticize and
it's different. I've found it's very different when you're in there having to
make the tough calls. (10/28/87, TX)

Thus, the candidates engaged in the three political campaign discourse
functions, focusing particularly on acclaims and, to a lesser extent, on
attacks. Table 6.1 displays the functions of this debate.

Topics of the 1987 Republican Debate

In this debate, character utterances (59%) were more common than
policy statements (41%). For instance, Robertson provided an example
of a character utterance when he talked about several qualities that were
important for a president to possess: "And I believe that for a man of
integrity and a man of courage and leadership is what we need as we
go into the next decade into the next century" (10/28/87, TX). On the
other hand, Kemp touted his future tax policy plans: "I would present
to the American people and have a comprehensive program to put a lid
on spending, provide the president with a line item veto, not raise taxes,
but cut the capital gains tax rate if we have to touch taxes" (10/28/87,
TX). So the candidates discussed both policy and character matters. See
Table 6.2

The candidates' discussion of policy themes was balanced, with 31%
of policy themes addressing past deeds, 33% future plans, and 36%
general goals. For instance, past deeds was the subject of Dole's acclaim
of his voting record on the abortion issue: "I've been supporting pro-life
positions since 1975, two years after Roe vs. Wade" (10/28/87, TX).
Kemp acclaimed his general goal of the development of an anti-ballistic
missile (ABM) system: "To rely on strategic defense, I think our party
ought to offer that [an ABM defense] to the American people in 1988"

TABLE 6.1
Functions of the 1987 Republican Debate

	Acclaims	Attacks	Defenses
Bush	80 (77%)	23 (22%)	1 (1%)
Dole	76 (85%)	13 (14%)	1 (1%)
DuPont	69 (73%)	25 (26%)	1 (1%)
Haig	51 (63%)	30 (37%)	0
Kemp	81 (74%)	28 (26%)	0
Robertson	68 (66%)	35 (34%)	0
Total	425 (73%)	154 (26%)	3 (1%)

TABLE 6.2
Topics of the 1987 Republican Debate

	Policy	Character
Bush	44 (43%)	59 (57%)
Dole	28 (31%)	61 (69%)
DuPont	46 (49%)	48 (51%)
Haig	27 (33%)	54 (67%)
Kemp	50 (46%)	59 (54%)
Robertson	44 (43%)	59 (57%)
Total	239 (41%)	340 (59%)

(10/28/87, TX). Pat Robertson acclaimed a potential future plan: "As president I would guarantee a veto of any appropriations measure which included one dime of funding for planned parenthood" (10/28/87, TX). Policy utterances were fairly evenly distributed in the 1987 debate between the three categories. See Table 6.3.

Discussion of ideals was the most frequent character theme of the Republican debate. Twenty-one percent of character themes concerned personal qualities, 25% addressed leadership ability, and 54% referred to ideals. George Bush acclaimed his personal qualities when he said, "But as I said, said to your friend Sam Donaldson a few years ago, in our family, loyalty is a strength, not a character flaw" (10/28/87, TX). Dole acclaimed his leadership ability in this passage: "What America wants is leadership, someone who can work with the Congress, someone who can get things done, and I'm willing to take on that responsibility" (10/28/87, TX). In another instance, Kemp acclaimed his ideals when he said, "I am convinced that we're entering an age in which we

TABLE 6.3
Forms of Policy and Character in the 1987 Republican Debate

	Policy						Character					
	Past Deeds*		Future Plans		General Goals		Personal Qualities		Leadership Ability		Ideals	
Bush	9	2	8	7	15	3	16	9	16	0	16	2
Dole	8	6	2	1	9	2	8	1	20	2	29	1
DuPont	2	2	21	3	12	6	3	1	3	0	28	13
Haig	4	4	1	5	10	3	12	2	16	8	8	8
Kemp	9	5	9	7	16	4	1	2	5	4	41	6
Robertson	2	21	10	4	6	1	15	2	11	0	24	7
Total	34	40	51	27	68	19	55	17	71	14	146	37
	74		78		87		72		85		183	
	31%		33%		36%		21%		25%		54%	

*Acclaims/attacks.

have some stark choices, but there are problems in this country that we can't resolve working together" (10/28/87, TX). Ideals were the most frequently mentioned character qualities.

Target of Attack in the 1987 Republican Debate

These candidates frequently attacked those within their own party (63%), with a few attacks directed toward the Democrats (8%) or the status quo (30%). These data are displayed in Table 6.4. In the 1988 Texas Republican debate, there were many instance of attack on members of the Republican Party. For instance, DuPont attacked Dole for his ideas on the national budget deficit: "With respect to my friend Dole, putting off curing the United States budget deficit until they do something in Japan is just plain nonsense" (10/28/87, TX). The Republican candidates also attacked members of the other party. For example, Dole attacked members of the Democratic Party on the Anti-Ballistic Missile Treaty: "I don't think there's any question about it. What we've got to worry about are some in the other party who are trying to restrict the interpretation of the ABM so much and so tight" (10/28/87, TX). The status quo was also the target of attacks. For instance, Robertson attacked the general moral environment: "I think we have a serious moral crisis in America" (10/28/87, TX). He did not attribute this problem to any particular target. It is notable that so many of these attacks, however, were directed toward members of their own party.

Issues Addressed in the 1987 Republican Debate

A public opinion poll administered near the date of the Republican debate revealed that the public thought the most important issue in the race at that time was the federal deficit, followed by employment, taxes,

TABLE 6.4
Target of Attack in the 1987 Republican Debate

| | Own Party (Republicans) | | | | | | | Dem. | Establish-ment |
	Bush	Dole	DuPont	Haig	Kemp	Rob.	Repub. General		
Bush	—	1	7	8	1	1	1	0	4
Dole	0	—	0	0	1	0	4	4	1
DuPont	8	2	—	0	2	0	7	1	5
Haig	2	1	0	—	0	0	13	1	6
Kemp	4	3	8	0	—	0	7	3	3
Robertson	2	0	0	0	0	—	7	2	24
Total	16	7	15	8	4	1	39	11	43
	90 (63%)							(8%)	(30%)

education, and relations with the Soviet Union. The largest segment of remarks, 44%, addressed issues other than those most important to voters. However, at times these candidates did discuss the matters that were uppermost in the mind of the public. For example, Kemp addressed the deficit in this acclaim: "I would present to the American people and have a comprehensive program to put a lid on spending" (10/28/87, TX). Employment was discussed by Bush in Texas, when he declared, "I've talked about creating more jobs." Kemp talked about taxes when he explained, "I am convinced that this president ought to veto any tax bill coming out of Congress" (10/28/87, TX). Education also surfaced in the debate. For example, DuPont advocated more support for private schools, which "means a voucher system that puts competition into schools" (10/28/87, TX). Haig expressed concern over the INF Treaty: "It ignores the fact that the Soviet Union is continuing to conduct aggression around the world and that we have delinked, so to speak, their international behavior from arms control in a quest for arms control for arms control sake" (10/28/87, TX). These excerpts illustrate how these candidates addressed these issues in the debates. See Table 6.5.

Most of the candidates spoke at least occasionally on these issues, except for Haig (who discussed only four of the six policy topics). However, Haig devoted more remarks than any other candidate to the topic that ranked first with voters, the deficit. Apart from "other" issues, Bush addressed Soviet relations most often, followed by the issues of taxes and education. Bush infrequently talked about taxes and never about the federal deficit. Dole spent most of his time on issues that were not most important to the public. Soviet relations and tax issues were discussed second most often by Dole, followed by the deficit. Dole also discussed jobs and education less frequently. DuPont also devoted most of his remarks to issues other than those valued by

TABLE 6.5
Issues Addressed in the 1987 Republican Debate

	Deficit 25%	Jobs 14%	Taxes 12%	Education 9%	Soviet Relations 9%	Other 31%
Bush	0	1	3	3	7	9
Dole	2	1	4	1	4	8
DuPont	1	1	2	4	4	15
Haig	4	0	0	1	8	2
Kemp	3	2	5	0	5	14
Robertson	3	1	2	4	4	14
Total	13 (9%)	6 (4%)	16 (11%)	13 (9%)	32 (23%)	62 (44%)

Gallup, 1988.

the public. Then he addressed education and Soviet relations, followed by taxes, then jobs and the deficit. Haig was the only candidate to discuss Soviet relations more than any other issue. He discussed the deficit, issues other than those included in the poll, and education, in that order. Kemp also addressed other issues, followed by taxes and Soviet relations, the deficit, and jobs. Pat Robertson discussed other issues most frequently, followed by education and Soviet relations, the deficit, employment, and taxes, respectively. Thus, all of the candidates except Haig devoted most of their remarks to issues that were at the top of the public's concerns. There was little relationship between the public's evaluation of important policy issues and the frequency with which the Republican candidates discussed those issues.

Bush, the sitting vice president, initially lost the Iowa caucus to both Robert Dole and Pat Robertson. However, a win in New Hampshire and South Carolina propelled Bush solidly to the front-runner status (Kendall, 2000). He picked Dan Quayle as a running mate and went on to win the 1988 general election.

THE DEMOCRATS

The campaign for the primary was a contentious race for the Democrats. In May 1987, Gary Hart, a favored candidate, withdrew from the race after the mass media reported Hart's marital infidelities, although he reentered the race by the spring of 1988. This left a field of candidates vying for the Democratic nomination, including the civil rights leader Jesse Jackson, Senator Paul Simon from Illinois, Senator Al Gore from Tennessee, and Michael Dukakis, the governor of Massachusetts. The texts used are from one debate held at the Iowa State Fair in Des Moines in August 1987, and the other is from Des Moines on January 15, 1988. Data from both debates are included in these analyses.

Functions of the 1987–1988 Democratic Debates

In these Democratic debates, acclaims (65%) were the most frequently enacted function. For instance, Gore acclaimed his policy position on arms control and other policy issues: "Let me single out one related policy that I think deserves more attention. In each year's budget we're devoting enormous funds to the arms race. If the next President can seek a verifiable and meaningful arms control agreement, we can redirect large sums of money away from the arms race and toward deficit reduction, investments in environmental protection and health care, and education" (1/15/88, IA). Attacks (32%) were the second most frequent function. Gephardt provided an example of an attack when he attacked the administration: "This administration expresses a value of survival of the fittest, selfishness. That the society, the government, has no role in organizing, in harmonizing, in the making the economy work for the people of this country" (1/15/88, IA). Defenses comprised 3% of the utterances in these debates. For instance, at one point, Dukakis defended the economic performance of Massachusetts against Senator Simon. "Well as you know, Paul, only about five percent of the new jobs we have created in the past ten years are defense related, so most of the jobs that we have in my state have very little to do with defense, those that we've added" (1/15/88, IA). Thus, in these debates, acclaims were more frequent than attacks, and attacks were more frequent than defenses. Table 6.6 shows the distribution of these functions.

Topics of the 1987–1988 Democratic Debates

In the 1988 Democratic debates, policy utterances (72%) were much more frequent than character (28%). For instance, the fiscal policies of the status quo were attacked. Simon attacked the tax policies of the status quo: "While the very wealthy of this nation had their taxes reduced, one third of middle income America, including a lot of Iowa farmers, really got gouged with that tax bill" (1/15/88, IA). Character issues were discussed less frequently. In the second Iowa debate, Jackson declared, "There is no substitute for courageous leadership" (1/15/88, IA). The results of this analysis are displayed in Table 6.7.

The candidates' discussion of policy themes favored those about past deeds: 43% of policy themes addressed past deeds. In one instance, Simon acclaimed his voting record: Simon argued, "That tax bill was a monster, and I am proud to have voted against it" (1/15/88, IA). Future plans made up 8% of policy utterances. For instance, Simon acclaimed

TABLE 6.6
Functions of the 1987–1988 Democratic Debates

	Acclaims	Attacks	Defenses
Babbitt	62 (64%)	33 (34%)	2 (2%)
Biden	29 (62%)	17 (36%)	1 (2%)
Dukakis	92 (70%)	37 (28%)	3 (2%)
Gephardt	65 (69%)	39 (36%)	6 (5%)
Gore	73 (63%)	39 (34%)	4 (3%)
Hart	49 (65%)	26 (34%)	1 (1%)
Jackson	81 (64%)	43 (34%)	3 (2%)
Simon	83 (75%)	24 (21%)	5 (4%)
Total	534 (65%)	258 (32%)	25 (3%)

TABLE 6.7
Topics of the 1987–1988 Democratic Debates

	Policy	Character
Babbitt	65 (68%)	30 (32%)
Biden	33 (72%)	13 (28%)
Dukakis	87 (67%)	42 (33%)
Gephardt	76 (73%)	28 (27%)
Gore	87 (78%)	25 (22%)
Hart	54 (72%)	21 (28%)
Jackson	88 (71%)	36 (29%)
Simon	79 (74%)	28 (26%)
Total	569 (72%)	223 (28%)

a specific plan for nuclear testing policy: "But in response to those three specific needs, let me ask my colleagues on this panel this afternoon if we couldn't agree this afternoon to do these three things. Number one, no matter which one of us is elected President, on January 21, 1989, if the Soviets will agree, we will stop all nuclear testing. It's verifiable, it would be a significant step away from the arms race" (1/15/88, IA). General goals (49%) were also discussed in these Democratic debates. Simon addressed the general goal of quality long-term, universal care when he suggested, "Let's pledge that we will have a self-financed program that moves on the problems of long-term care for all older Americans" (1/15/88, IA). The Democrats used all three forms of policy utterances.

The largest group of character themes concerned personal qualities (49%), with less emphasis on leadership ability (23%) and ideals (28%). Babbitt posed this as an important question for voters: "Are candidates really worthy of our trust?" (1/15/88, IA). Leadership ability was the form of 23% of Democratic character utterances. Babbitt acclaimed his leadership ability in the earlier debate: "During my time in Arizona, I made a special effort to lead rural development. And what I learned was that diversification is possible" (7/23/87, IA). Ideals were also a prominent form of character utterances. Gephardt took up a matter of principle when he declared, "So it goes to a real question of values, of standing up for the rights of people" (1/15/88, IA). So the Democratic candidates discussed both policy and character in these debates. See Table 6.8.

Target of Attack in the 1987–1988 Democratic Debates

The Democratic candidates attacked the Republicans (58%) more than other Democrats (14%) or the status quo (28%). For instance, in the

TABLE 6.8
Forms of Policy and Character in the 1987–1988 Democratic Debates

	Policy						Character					
	Past Deeds		Future Plans		General Goals		Personal Qualities		Leadership Ability		Ideals	
Babbitt	3	19	5	4	31	3	10	6	6	0	7	1
Biden	1	16	0	0	15	1	8	0	2	0	3	0
Dukakis	8	31	3	1	44	0	18	1	13	4	6	0
Gephardt	11	25	7	0	30	3	10	5	3	1	4	5
Gore	2	27	3	4	46	5	7	3	6	0	9	0
Hart	6	22	0	0	26	0	9	3	0	0	8	1
Jackson	15	33	0	1	39	1	14	1	5	7	8	1
Simon	9	20	16	0	33	1	14	1	4	1	7	1
Total	55	193	34	10	264	14	90	20	39	13	52	9
	43%		8%		49%		49%		23%		28%	

*Acclaims/attacks.

second debate, Dukakis attacked the Reagan-Bush administration: "And that very, very serious and destructive fiscal policy, which began in the early eighties under this administration, has done a terrible job on manufacturing, on our basic industries, on our ability to compete, whether it's our farmers who are trying to export or our manufacturing industries who are trying to stay competitive" (1/15/88, IA). The Democratic candidates also attacked each other. For instance, Gore attacked the general goals of Dukakis's economic plans: "And I also heard something else that you said which I disagree with. You said, you said we must raise revenue. You said we must raise revenue. Now, if we have a recession when the next President takes office in January of 1989, that would be the very worst thing to do" (7/27/87, IA). The status quo was also attacked in these debates. Biden, for instance, attacked the farm policy of the status quo: "The people are not out of business because they are bad businessmen and bad farmers. They are out of business because of bad farm policy and I think they should get the chance, not some cartel out of Chicago, or New York, or Los Angeles, at that lower interest rate" (7/27/87, IA). Thus, while the status quo and other Democratic candidates were the target of some attacks, Republicans were the primary target of attacks. These data are displayed in Table 6.9.

Issues Addressed in the 1987–1988 Democratic Debates

We used public opinion poll data to establish which issues were most important to voters at the time of these debates (note that respondents were allowed more than one response in this poll). The largest number of utterances (37%) were devoted to topics other than those that were

TABLE 6.9
Target of Attack in the 1987–1988 Democratic Debates

	Own Party (Democrats)									Repub.	Establish-ment
	Bab.	Bid.	Duk.	Gep.	Gore	Hart	Jack.	Sim.	Dem.		
Babbitt	—	0	1	5	0	0	0	0	1	12	13
Biden	0	—	0	0	0	0	0	1	1	8	7
Dukakis	0	0	—	1	1	0	0	0	2	28	6
Gephardt	0	0	0	—	1	0	0	0	0	25	14
Gore	4	2	0	4	—	0	2	1	2	19	5
Hart	0	0	0	0	0	—	0	0	2	23	0
Jackson	1	0	0	0	0	0	—	0	2	24	18
Simon	0	0	0	0	0	0	0	—	3	11	10
Totals	35									150	73
	(14%)									(58%)	(28%)

most important to the public. However, at times these candidates did discuss the issues that mattered most to voters. Dukakis, for example, discussed the economy in this statement: The future "[a]nti-trust policy is one of the most important things we have in this country, to ensure competitive, free enterprise economy, something that we Democrats are for and very strongly so" (1/15/88, IA). Biden was one candidate who discussed problems of the Reagan administration when he declared:

> The first [reason we have done well in the past] is that every generation of Americans has understood that its responsibility was to leave a legacy to the succeeding generation, that was in fact better and more prosperous than the one that they inherited. Now we're not doing that now under the Reagan administration. Under the Reagan administration we are leaving our children with a close to three trillion dollar debt. We are making it harder for them to get to college. We are shortening their possibilities, rather than lengthening them. (7/27/87, IA)

Foreign policy was also important to many voters. Gephardt addressed American policy in Central America: "It is wrong, it's just plain wrong, to be spending millions of dollars on mercenary soldiers in Nicaragua who are killing children when we don't have enough money in our own budget to help children here in the United States" (7/27/87, IA). Jackson brought up employment we he asserted, "There's thirty-eight million jobs leaving this economy" (7/27/87, IA). Education was discussed by Gephardt in this excerpt: "The first thing we've got to do is to educate our people, make them strong, invest in people. The 25% dropout rate in our schools is a disaster, and it's got to be turned around" (7/27/87, IA). Thus, these passages illustrate how the candidates addressed the issues that mattered most to the public. This information is displayed in Table 6.10.

Babbitt discussed the economy and issues not included on the survey most frequently, followed by problems with the present administration, foreign policy, education, and employment issues, in that order. Biden addressed the economy most frequently, then employment and issues not mentioned in the survey. Biden also mentioned education and flaws in the Reagan administration, respectively. Dukakis discussed issues other than those identified by voters most frequently. Dukakis discussed the economy second most frequently, followed by problems with the Reagan administration, employment issues and education, followed by foreign policy. Gephardt also mentioned issues other than those judged most important in the poll most frequently. Gephardt discussed the economy second most frequently, then problems in the Republican administration, education, foreign policy, and employment issues less frequently. Gore discussed the economy most often. Gore discussed issues other than those identified in the poll second most often, followed by flaws in the current administration, education, employment, and foreign policy, in that order of utterance frequency. Hart discussed issues not identified in the survey most often, followed by problems in the Republican administration, education, foreign policy, the economy, and employment, in that order. Jackson addressed other issues most often, followed by the economy. Jackson mentioned foreign policy, employment issues, and education an equal number of times. Less often, Jackson discussed problems with the Reagan administration. Simon addressed the economy most frequently. Simon addressed other issues second most frequently, followed by the failures of the

TABLE 6.10
Issues Addressed in the 1987–1988 Democratic Debates

	Economy (48%)	Present Admin. (38%)	Foreign Policy (31%)	Jobs/ Wages (16%)	Education (14%)	Other (18%)
Babbitt	31	13	6	1	4	31
Biden	27	1	0	3	2	3
Dukakis	23	11	5	8	8	37
Gephardt	24	11	5	3	9	35
Gore	41	15	1	3	10	37
Hart	4	20	6	1	10	41
Jackson	19	8	12	12	12	38
Simon	30	10	8	1	8	28
Total	199 (29%)	89 (13%)	43 (6%)	32 (5%)	63 (9%)	250 (37%)

Cambridge Reports, 1988.
Note: Survey asked respondents to identify the two most important problems.

Reagan administration, education and foreign policy the same number of times, and employment issues least frequently. Thus, no Democratic candidate was clearly superior in addressing the issues that mattered most to the public.

Dukakis rose to the top of the Democratic field in the 1988 primary race, largely due to his claim that he had led Massachusetts to an economic revival. However, Dukakis displayed bland personal qualities. Ultimately, Michael Dukakis secured the Democratic nomination, but then George Bush defeated him in the general election. The word "liberal" was used incessantly by the Bush administration in attacks on the Massachusetts governor. The Bush campaign was very negative at points (for instance, the Willie Horton advertisements), although listless responses by the uncharismatic Dukakis did not help the Democratic campaign. Bush won 54% of the popular vote and 426 electoral votes, as opposed to Dukakis's 46% and 111 electoral votes (Brinkley, 1985). Study of these three debates through a functional approach has increased our understanding of the development of this dynamic discourse through the 1988 primary season.

REPUBLICANS VERSUS DEMOCRATS

This section will compare the Republican and Democratic debates analyzed for 1988. First, we discuss functions, then topics, then target of attacks, and finally issues addressed.

Functions of the 1988 Debates

The distribution of functions was different between the candidates of the two parties in the 1988 primary debates. Candidates from both parties acclaimed more than attacked or defended. A chi-square revealed that there was a significant difference between Republicans and Democrats and their use of functions ($\chi^2[df = 2] = 16.9$, $p < .001$). Republicans (73%) and Democrats (65%) both acclaimed more than they attacked. However, Democrats were more likely to attack (32%) and defend (3%) than Republicans (26% attack, 1% defend). The Republican Party held the White House in 1988, and it is possible that the Democrats tended to attack more because they were the challenging party.

Topics of the 1988 Debates

Republicans and Democrats differed significantly in their selection of topics ($\chi^2[df = 1] = 129.0$, $p < .001$). Republicans discussed character (59%) more than policy (41%), whereas Democrats discussed policy

(72%) more than character (28%). It is possible that the incumbent party was reluctant to discuss policy as much as the challengers.

There were differences between the Republican and Democratic candidates in the frequency of the forms of policy utterances. For instance, there was a significant difference between Republicans and Democrats and their use of past deeds (χ^2[df = 1] = 15.9, p < .001). Republicans acclaimed (34 utterances) and attacked (40) somewhat equally, whereas Democrats attacked (193) far more than they acclaimed (55). Clearly, some of this disparity was attributable to the fact that the Republicans already controlled the White House with Reagan. There was no significant difference between Republicans and Democrats and future plans (χ^2[df = 1] = 1.9, n.s.). A significant difference between Republicans and Democrats was found in their use of general goals (χ^2[df = 1] = 22.8, p < .001). While both Republicans and Democrats both acclaimed general goals more than they attacked, Democrats (264) acclaimed general goals to a much greater extent than Republicans (68). Attacks on general goals occurred at similar levels (Democrats: 14; Republicans: 19).

There were no significant differences between the Republicans and Democrats in their discussion of character. Specifically, Republicans and Democrats did not significantly differ in their discussion of personal qualities (χ^2[df = 1] = .79, n.s.). There was no significant difference between Republicans and Democrats and their use of leadership abilities (χ^2[df = 1] = 1.5, n.s.). No significant difference between Republicans and Democrats was found in their discussion of ideals (χ^2[df = 1] = .89, n.s.). Thus, this distribution did not vary due to party but rather as a function of primary debate discourse.

Target of Attacks in the 1988 Debates

In these debates, the Democratic candidates devoted most attacks to the other party (58%), the incumbent Republican Party (and 14% to each other). The Republicans, in contrast, devoted 65% of their attacks to each other (and 8% to the Democrats). The status quo received 27% of the Republican and 28% of the Democratic attacks. A chi-square reveals that there is a significant difference in target of attacks by political party (χ^2[df = 2] = 131.7, p < .001). It is possible that these results again reflect the fact that the Democrats were the challenging party, focusing much of their efforts on the incumbent administration.

Issues Addressed in the 1988 Debates

Republican policy utterances were allocated in this order: Other, 5th, 3rd, 1st, 4th, 2nd. Democratic policy remarks were apportioned in this order: Other, 1st, 2nd, 5th, 3rd, 4th. Thus, both parties devoted most policy comments to topics other than the top five issues to voters. However, after that, only one issue in the Democratic debates was not discussed in the order of importance for voters: The issue that ranked 5th to voters was discussed 3rd most frequently (after "other"). So the Democrats did a better job addressing the issues that were most important to voters in their debates.

CONCLUSION

In conclusion, study of the 1987–1988 primary debates indicates that the functions of these primary debates are consistent with the characteristics of primary debates throughout this study. However, regularities that emerge throughout this longitudinal study reveal that primary debates do perform a distinct distribution of functions.

7

1992: Who Will Challenge the Leader of Desert Storm?

The 1992 election became memorable to the nation as several sayings entered into our national vocabulary. We learned the value of the economy with the saying "It's the economy, stupid." The words "read my lips" became synonymous with a lie. Then we learned that there was no harm in experimenting with marijuana as long was we "did not inhale." These sayings crept into our minds during the 1992 election, and there would be more to come with Bill Clinton's presidency. In this chapter we will explore the 1992 Democratic primary debates that helped to bring about that memorable election. First, we will begin with a brief sketch of the participants, followed by a recap of the primaries, and finally a functional analysis of three March debates. All will help to explain why 1992 was so memorable.

BACKGROUND OF THE 1992 DEMOCRATIC DEBATES

Five men contested the 1992 Democratic nomination. Former California Governor Jerry Brown, who ran as a Washington outsider, wanted to purge the government of the "money grubbing politicians" (Carlson, 1992, p. 27). Brown tried to identify with the voters as the only candidate who was "as disaffected as they are" with the state of the nation (p. 27). The second option was Arkansas Governor Bill Clinton who was seen as more electable than a traditional liberal Democrat (Church, 1992). He was described as "a Southerner who took many moderate stands on— education and welfare reform, for example, and talked constantly about the 'responsibility' of people who receive government benefits to do something in return" (p. 22). The third choice was Iowa Senator Tom Harkin, who "proclaimed himself 'the only real Democrat in the race' and said his rivals were 'all just shades of Republican policies' " (Barrett, 1992a, p. 22). The fourth candidate, Nebraska Senator Bob Kerrey, was similar to Harkin. He used his military status, his health care reform plan, and his midwestern Nebraska values to help his campaign (Barrett, 1992a, pp. 22–23). The final Democratic candidate was former Senator Paul Tsongas of Massachusetts, who had recovered from cancer and had a message that he thought all would be receptive to, no matter who the source (Allis, 1992, p. 26).

Prior to the election season of 1992, the Democratic Party did not seem to have a viable candidate to offer to the American public. "Democrats were a party in despair. Election year was imminent, but they had little to say, and no candidate to say it powerfully" ("Clinton's Message," 1992, p. 13). Despite the early fears of Democrats, the election year ended with the defeat of President George Bush and the first of eight years with President Bill Clinton. While Clinton would defeat Bush, he had to first emerge as a viable option among the Democratic hopefuls and then set his sights on Bush.

The 1992 primary season began in Iowa on February 10, 1992, with their caucuses. Senator Tom Harkin of Iowa won the caucus, but no other candidate emerged strongly. While Harkin did win, only a poor showing by him would have been newsworthy if his home state rejected him. The second-place finish of "Mr. Undecided, who got 12%, or more than all other candidates put together" ("From Sea," 1992, p. 26), made New Hampshire's February 18th primary loom even more important than previously believed. It was thought "whoever wins or does well there will gather valuable 'momentum' and media attention. But his task is only beginning" ("From Sea," 1992, p. 26). After Iowa, Paul Tsongas became Clinton's primary challenger (Barrett, 1992b). Although Tsongas won in New Hampshire, none of the five candidates emerged from that primary with a sizable lead over the other candidates. Clinton appeared to be losing appeal due to accusations of being a "draft dodger" and a "womanizer." Tsongas used his win to help demonstrate his ability to move away from being viewed as only "a regional New England candidate" and toward being viewed as someone who has the stamina to survive a national race (Church, 1992, p. 22). The two Farm Belt candidates, Harkin and Kerrey, failed to strike an interest in the voters of New England and appeared to be losing any momentum they may once have had in the race. Finally, "Jerry Brown still looked to be in a private orbit somewhere" (Church, 1992, p. 22). After New Hampshire, South Dakota provided the next opportunity to limit the field. The third-place finish by Kerrey in New Hampshire was erased by the nearly "40% of the South Dakota Democratic vote" from his neighboring state ("Heartburn in the Heartland," 1992, p. 26). The same day as South Dakota were the Maine caucuses where "Jerry Brown, whom it suits none of the other candidates to take seriously, almost beat Mr. Tsongas" ("Heartburn in the Heartland," 1992, p. 26). The early states failed to decrease the drama of the Democratic Party where no "true" front-runner emerged from the pack.

Bill Clinton's turn in the spotlight came on Super Tuesday, when he emerged as the candidate for the party. The 11 states voting on March 10th helped to propel Clinton to the front of the Democratic Party and began to eliminate the other candidates who realized they had no more chance at the nomination. Even more importance was placed on Super Tuesday after Bush's battles with Pat Robertson for the extreme Right of the Republican Party. Pat Robertson's campaign demonstrated that Bush could be defeated, and there was blood in the water. Clinton's 52% to 34% win over Tsongas in Florida moved him closer to the Democratic prize ("The Fine Old Contest," 1992, p. 25). The Super Tuesday wins were needed for Clinton to move from being the southerner to being a viable candidate. The contests in Illinois and Michigan would demonstrate his ability as a national candidate. The best opportunity to slow down Clinton's campaign was Michigan, where "many union bosses, supporters of Tom Harkin before he bowed out of the race, are urging workers to vote for uncommitted delegates" ("Moody Michigan," 1992, p. 26). Clinton "trounced his remaining two rivals so badly during crucial primaries in Illinois and Michigan last week that Paul Tsongas suspended his campaign, leaving only Jerry Brown still snapping at his heels" (Hull, 1992, 20). The once five-person race was then reduced to a two-person race, but in reality the nomination was Clinton's.

Jerry Brown stayed in the race because his campaign was more of an indictment of the current state of politics. Brown could not have beaten Clinton after late March, but he could "bruise him badly, doing the work for the Republicans all the way through the convention" (Hull, 1992, p. 22). Unlike Brown, Tsongas bowed out since he "would have helped George Bush win another White House tour had he stayed in the race. 'The alternative was clear . . . I did not survive my ordeals in order to be the agent of the re-election of George Bush' " (Allis, 1992, p. 26). A race between Clinton and Brown made most Democratic leaders "obliged to put aside their concerns about [Clinton's] electability and fall in behind him" (Hull, 1992, p. 25). Finally, Bill Clinton did gain the Democratic nomination and defeated Bush in the November election to become the 42nd president.

The three debates selected from the 1992 debates all occurred in March as the race began to move in Clinton's favor. The March 1, 1992, Atlanta, Georgia (3/1/92, GA), debate was attended by Brown, Clinton,

Kerrey, and Tsongas. The March 5, 1992, Dallas, Texas (3/5/92,TX), debate was attended by Brown, Clinton, Harkin, and Tsongas. The March 27, 1992, St. Paul, Minnesota (3/27/92, MN), debate only included Brown and Clinton, because the other three candidates had dropped out by then. These three debates included all five of the candidates, and they also reflected the changing face of the Democratic primary.

FUNCTIONS OF THE 1992 DEMOCRATIC DEBATES

Understanding the 1992 debates begins with the functions of utterances made by the five candidates, which were dominated by acclaims. As stated earlier, acclaims show the candidate in a favorable light. Acclaims can also help to define a candidate to the voters so that he or she will appear preferable to opponents. In these three debates under examination, the candidates focused on acclaims (65%). Bill Clinton provided an acclaim when he lauded the importance of education and his work in that arena: "I believe that presidents can do a great deal to improve the educational system, and I think it's terribly important. I've worked very hard for the last eleven years to upgrade the schools, the colleges, the universities, the training programs in my state" (3/27/92, MN). In this instance he showed how he is preferable by declaring his long-term commitment to education and his positive 11-year history of improvement in Arkansas. See Table 7.1.

While acclaims help to show the good the candidate has done or will do, candidates also attack their opposition. In these debates, attacks were the second most common function (32%). Brown's critique of Clinton's proposed health care reforms provided an example of a common attack: "The trouble I see with Governor Clinton's program is that it's going to create different levels of care. And I'm afraid that poor people are going to get the short end, as they always do, because of their lack of political power" (3/27/92, MN). In this statement, Brown spe-

TABLE 7.1
Functions of the 1992 Democratic Debates

	Acclaims	Attacks	Defenses
Brown	305 (62%)	178 (36%)	9 (2%)
Clinton	382 (69%)	155 (28%)	16 (3%)
Harkin	29 (52%)	24 (43%)	3 (5%)
Kerrey	48 (69%)	18 (26%)	4 (6%)
Tsongas	50 (60%)	27 (33%)	6 (7%)
Total	814 (65%)	402 (32%)	38 (3%)

cifically attacked the Clinton plan for not adequately protecting poor people. If Brown can decrease Clinton's desirability, Brown will look better in comparison.

The third function of campaign discourse is defense, which is a specific response to an attack made by another candidate. A defense works to show that the candidate is not as undesirable as another candidate has claimed. In these three debates defenses accounted for relatively few remarks (3%). The Texas debate featured an attack by Harkin on Brown that questioned the number of contributors to his campaign. Brown's response was that "I've got 35,000 contributors, I'll tell you this" (3/5/92, TX). Provision of the actual number of contributors functioned to deny Harkin's attack on relatively little support for Brown. The low occurrence of defenses could be explained since the time spent to respond to the attack was time diverted away from the message of "elect me." Acclaims and attacks both speak that message, but the defense diverts the speaker away from the larger message of why he or she is the best person to represent the party for president.

TOPICS OF THE 1992 DEMOCRATIC DEBATES

Statements can address either policy or character. Policy statements concern problems and government actions, such as providing a new health care plan or setting up a new arms control agreement. Questions of character deal with the characteristics of the candidate as a person, such as honesty, courage, compassion, leadership ability, principles, or core values.

The 1992 debates were dominated by discussion of policy. The three debates featured many policy utterances (68%); fewer than half that many utterances were devoted to character (32%). For example, in the Minnesota debate, Clinton acclaimed his plan to "put one person in charge of fighting the battle against AIDS." (3/27/92, MN). Contrast that discussion of proposed governmental policy with Brown's description of the qualities he esteems: "I believe that what we need is honesty and simplicity and to recapture those basic values of our American society" (3/27/92, MN). Thus, the candidates addressed both character and policy in these debates. See Table 7.2.

Each of the two topics then can be broken into three different forms of utterances. Beginning with the policy statement, a rhetor can make a statement of either a past deed, a future plan, or a general goal. When making a character statement, one can discuss leadership ability, personal qualities, or ideals. These six options can take the form of either an acclaim or an attack by the rhetor.

TABLE 7.2
Topics of the 1992 Democratic Debates

	Policy	Character
Brown	288 (60%)	195 (40%)
Clinton	400 (72%)	157 (28%)
Harkin	44 (83%)	9 (17%)
Kerrey	52 (80%)	13 (20%)
Tsongas	58 (68%)	27 (32%)
Total	842 (68%)	401 (32%)

Beginning with the policy forms, the candidate can make a statement about his or her past deeds. The past deed refers to accomplishments or actions that have been done that help to provide empirical proof of the capability of the candidate to be the president. In these three 1992 debates, 38 acclaims of past deeds were made, and 184 attacks were made, accounting for 26% of the policy utterances. Paul Tsongas attacked the Republican Party's handling of defense spending when he stated: "The thing of the danger of what Reagan and Bush have done, is they went through this massive increase in defense spending, and now that we end up with the cold war over and this contraction taking place, they have not provided the mechanism for new companies to start up, to employ people who are going to desperately need that employment" (3/5/92, TX). Here the past deed refers to Reagan and Bush's increased military spending accompanied by the lack of initiative for a peacetime economy plan by the two presidents. See Table 7.3.

The second form of policy is the future plan, which explains the means the candidate proposes for improving matters. Just as with past deeds, future plans can be either acclaims or attacks. The 1992 debates made 254 future plan acclaims and only 67 future plan attacks,

TABLE 7.3
Forms of Policy and Character in the 1992 Democratic Debates

	Policy						Character					
	Past Deeds*		Future Plans		General Goals		Personal Qualities		Leadership Ability		Ideals	
Brown	8	91	76	16	90	7	12	8	16	9	103	47
Clinton	25	63	131	35	132	14	24	9	23	6	67	28
Harkin	4	15	9	3	10	3	2	1	1	2	3	0
Kerrey	0	4	20	7	21	0	2	7	1	0	3	0
Tsongas	1	11	18	6	15	6	7	7	5	1	6	1
Total	38	184	254	67	268	30	47	32	46	18	182	76
	26%		38%		35%		20%		16%		64%	

*Acclaims/attacks.

accounting for 38% of all policy utterances. Kerrey provided an example of an acclaiming future plan: "My proposal will cost an average American $500 less a year, but it will allow us to focus on job training and education" (3/1/92, GA). It is clear that Kerrey has a specific plan for achieving this benefit. While Kerrey acclaimed, Clinton and Brown attacked each other over specifics of their health care and tax plans. Clinton attacked Brown's tax plan by saying, "The third thing I don't like about it is, according to everyone who's analyzed it, it won't raise enough money to cover current spending, so it adds $180 billion to the deficit" (3/27/92, MN). Here Clinton attacked the specifics of Brown's tax plan and argued that it would substantially worsen the deficit.

The final option for the form of policy is the general goal. General goals are more vague or abstract than future plans, stressing the ends rather than the specific means. Once again, a candidate can acclaim or attack general goals. The three debates utilized 268 general goal acclaims and 30 general goal attacks, constituting 35% of the policy utterances. Brown's plan to deal with nuclear energy articulated a general goal when he stated, "Yes, I would phase out nuclear power as it now is presently configured" (3/27/92, MN). This identified a goal that Brown wanted to accomplish as president, but he did not state how he would phase out nuclear power.

In addition to the three forms of policy utterance, there are also the three forms of a candidate's character utterances. The first form of character utterance is the statement about personal qualities. Personal qualities typically refer to the past experience, usually nongovernmental, a candidate possesses that will differ from the other candidates'. Again, personal qualities can be either acclaims or attacks. The 1992 debates included 47 acclaims and 32 attacks of personal qualities, which accounted for 20% of the total character utterances. Harkin provided an example of a discourse addressing personal qualities by saying that "it depends on who you are and how much guts you've got, and whether you've got the courage to stand up to people and fight for working people, for laboring people, for family farmers" (3/5/92, TX). He explicitly acclaims courage, and he clearly suggests that the president must care about ordinary people.

The second form of character utterance concerns the candidate's leadership ability. The 1992 debates included 46 acclaims and 18 attacks on leadership ability that accounted for 16% of the character utterances. Harkin attacked Brown's lack of leadership when he declared that "what we need is a president who hasn't been sitting on the sidelines, like you have been" (3/5/92, TX). Clearly, a leader must be active, working to accomplish desirable outcomes through governing. Similarly, Clinton attacked the incumbent Republican administration's lack of leadership when he declared, "We've lost our economic leadership" (3/1/92, GA). These utterances illustrate leadership themes.

The third character form is the ideal. Ideals are described as values or principles that ought to be held by people. The three debates we examined used 182 ideal acclaims and 76 ideal attacks (64%). Brown provided an example of the acclaiming ideal when he discussed the death penalty: "[T]hey have that right. Their local police that's their business, but the real issue is this gross injustice" (3/5/92, TX). Brown suggests that justice is an important value, and in fact it is more important than local control of police activities. Thus, these excerpts illustrate the candidates' use of the forms of policy and character in these debates.

TARGET OF ATTACK IN THE 1992 DEMOCRATIC DEBATES

The debates offer an opportunity for the candidates to level attacks upon their opponents. Attacks on the other candidates can occur due to the confrontational nature of debates themselves and because candidates can use attacks on others to show their differences. It should be noted that in these 1992 debates only Brown and Clinton participated in all three debates, whereas Tsongas appeared in two. Harkin and Kerrey each only appeared in one debate.

When candidates were given the opportunity to attack another candidate, Brown was on the receiving end more than the other four. Brown was the recipient of 48 attacks (46%) articulated by the other four candidates (see Table 7.4). For instance, Clinton repeatedly criticized Brown's tax proposal:

> Governor Brown put out a five page statement on this, he addressed this not at all, he didn't think through any of this. And I will quote again from the editorial writer of the *New York Daily News*, he said it would be the biggest ripoff on the average middle class taxpayer in the history of tax

TABLE 7.4
Target of Attack in the 1992 Democratic Debates

	Brown	Clinton	Harkin	Kerrey	Tsongas	Bush/GOP	Establishment
Brown	—	17	1	1	1	32	188
Clinton	36	—	1	4	8	37	67
Harkin	2	1	—	0	4	8	7
Kerrey	3	8	0	—	6	1	3
Tsongas	7	1	1	0	—	11	9
Total	48 (47%)	27 (26%)	3 (3%)	5 (5%)	19 (19%)	89 (19%)	274 (59%)
		102 (22%)					

policy. Even Ronald Reagan's tax people thought his proposal, the Brown proposal, was too reactionary. (3/27/92, MN)

Clinton intensified his attack by painting his fellow Democrat Brown as worse than one of the most conservative Republicans in recent history, Ronald Reagan.

While Brown was treated like a punching bag, Clinton received a share of the hits that were not intended for Brown. Clinton was the target of 26% of the attacks in these debates. Kerrey attacked Clinton's health care answer by stating that "that was a baloney answer. I mean, you're not going to be able to get a line appropriation to help every poor child in America get that kind of prenatal care" (3/1/92, GA). Here he rejects Clinton's health care proposal as unrealistic. Again, Clinton participated in all three debates, and he was the front-runner in March.

Fewer attacks were targeted at Tsongas, Harkin, and Kerrey than the other two candidates. Tsongas led the last three candidates with 18% of the attacks. For example, Brown attacked Tsongas's health care proposal by saying, "Well, I don't agree with Paul Tsongas' idea of managed competition. We've had experiments with that. Corporations are in business to make more and I think a major part of the problem with health care today is greed" (3/1/92, GA). Harkin (3 attacks) and Kerry (8 attacks), who each attended one of the debates we analyzed, were rarely attacked in these debates.

In addition to attacks on the other Democratic candidates, the Republicans also came under fire in these debates. The five Democrats advanced 89 attacks (19%) on Bush and the Republicans in the three debates. For instance, Tsongas attacked the Bush administration when he asked what they had done for an economic plan for the nation:

Well, during the Reagan-Bush years, the United States increasingly lost its capacity to compete. I mean, Japan has an economic strategy. Germany has an economic strategy. They know where they're going. Taiwan has an economic strategy. If you walk out here in the streets and ask anybody, "What is George Bush's economic battle plan to rescue this country?" they could not tell you. (3/5/92, TX)

The attack on Bush centered on his inability to rescue the economy from its current problems. Tsongas argued the lack of an administration plan was made worse because all of the other nations thought to be economically strong had plans but not the United States.

In addition to the attacks made on the other candidates and the opposition, attacks were also made on the establishment or the status quo. Attacks in this area could be seen as an attack on the political process in Washington, but they did not specifically designate one group as more to blame than the other group. The 1992 debates had 274 of these attacks. Brown accounted for the largest number of attacks (188) on the Washington system, mostly due to his attempt to run as the outsider: "The power in Washington is so out of touch that the basis of all this discussion is empty and meaningless unless you can find a way to create a political movement to move aside a corrupt status quo that is fed by thousand dollar donations and lobbying that is protected by this tax code that I'm attacking" (3/27/92, MN). Here Brown blamed all of Washington for the ills in government and called for some social movement, like his campaign, to change the problems in Washington. The problem with change is rooted in the ability to buy control over issues and to prevent change. Brown continued to blame many of the ills on the broken system in Washington and offered himself as an outsider who could change the system. These attacks by Brown continued to keep him on the outskirts of the Democratic Party, reinforcing his outsider status and legitimizing attacks on him by the other candidates. The other four candidates all made attacks against the establishment and the status quo, but none to the extent that Brown attacked. Attacks on the status quo or the establishment may not be harmful to the Democratic voters, but it might begin to paint a bleak picture for change.

ISSUES ADDRESSED IN THE 1992 DEMOCRATIC DEBATES

Public opinion polls were used to determine what issues were most important to the public. The first poll asked: "Are any of these issues so important to you that it will determine which presidential candidate you vote for?" (Gallup, 1992). The participants prior to all three of the debates could have seen this poll, so they had some idea of the topics that the voting public wanted to hear. The results from that survey indicated that the economy was the most important issue to the voting public (29%) (of the top five issues). The second was health care policy (15%), third was unemployment (14%), fourth was education (13%), and finally poverty and homelessness (12%) See Table 7.5.

First note that over half (54%) of the policy utterances in these debates addressed issues other than those that were the top issues in voters' minds. However, of the top five issues, the economy was discussed the most, in 107 utterances (24%). For instance, Clinton attacked the Bush administration's economic plan by saying: "Well, one reason for that uncertainty is that we are the only country in the world without any kind of national economic policy. We have no strategy to be a high-wage, high-growth country" (3/27/92, MN). Clinton's critique of the

TABLE 7.5
Issues Addressed in the 1992 Democratic Debates

	Economy (29%)	Health Care (15%)	Jobs (14%)	Education (13%)	Poverty/ Homeless (12%)	Other (17%)
Brown	24	14	9	7	0	88
Clinton	48	17	17	7	0	83
Harkin	18	0	5	0	0	21
Kerrey	1	18	6	0	0	27
Tsongas	16	5	6	0	0	32
Total	107 (23%)	54 (12%)	43 (9%)	14 (3%)	0	251 (54%)

Gallup, 2000.

lack of national economic policy helped to explain the economic troubles that were felt by the voting public in 1992. All five candidates discussed the economy, with Clinton and Brown discussing the economy the most. Kerrey only made one reference to the economy, and that might help to explain why he lacked support and had to drop out, since he almost entirely failed to discuss the issue. While Kerrey did not discuss the economy much, Clinton discussed the economy 48 times in his three debates. The top issue was actually addressed repeatedly by the five candidates.

The second-place issue of health care came in second with 54 remarks (12%). Tsongas addressed this issue by saying:

> Well, let's go from baloney to steak, if we can deal with this. I can't give you sizzle. I'll try to give the steak. The fact is that Bob Kerrey and I disagree on the issue of health care, but the fact is that the both of us have put together comprehensive plans. I care deeply about health care because I'm alive because of health care, and I feel what was available to me should be available to every American. (3/1/92, GA)

In this example, Tsongas began to talk about the general good of health care. He began to explain why he cares so much for health care due to his past health problems. For Tsongas, health care was important not only to the public but also to him. Only four of the five candidates mentioned health care. Kerrey made the most mentions of health care in the one debate he participated in, whereas Harkin failed to discuss health care. Despite the lower participation in health care discussion, it still remained the second most discussed issue.

The third-place issue to voters was jobs, and the candidates made 43 statements (10%) on this topic. For example, Kerrey discussed jobs when he declared: "In order to create jobs in the automobile industry, aerospace industry, semiconductor, rebuild our consumer electronics industry, we've got to shake this government to its foundation and take it and turn it and orient it, so that it now not only invests, but we have a coherent tax and regulatory policy, we've got a federal government that creates jobs someplace other than Washington D.C." (3/1/92, GA). Kerrey discussed the interrelationship between jobs and the economy. He was calling for a change in the government to assist the industrial base in the nation. Additionally, he was calling for the government to keep jobs in the United States and not lose companies to other nations. Just like the economy, every candidate made mention of jobs and employment in the three debates. Clinton did mention jobs more than the other candidates, with 17, but he participated in all three of the debates. All candidates averaged about 5 mentions of employment for each debate.

The fourth-place issue of importance to voters was education. In the debates the candidates made few statements (3%) about education. Despite being the fourth most important issue, only Brown and Clinton discussed education in the Minnesota debate. For example, Clinton described part of his goals for education in this passage: "I think we ought to have more funds to poor school districts and to low income kids concentrated especially on those early grades, giving schools, parents and give teachers the flexibility to use that money, particularly for smaller classes and elementary counselors in the early grades" (3/27/92, MN). Clinton's plan for education will help to focus on children at a younger age and in poorer districts. This educational plan will also help include the parents in the educational process, so it is not an exclusively governmental action. The lack of discussion by Harkin, Kerrey, and Tsongas might begin to explain why they dropped out in mid-March, since they did not address issues of importance to the voters. However, education only became an issue in the third debate when citizens of Minnesota and Wisconsin were able to question the candidates. Despite being the number-four issue in predebate polls, education was not an issue that the candidates chose to discuss extensively.

While the fourth most important issue was ignored until the third debate, the fifth issue was completely ignored in these debates. The predebate poll indicated poverty and homelessness constituted the fifth most important issue, but no candidate discussed the issue. Thus, these candidates devoted most of their remarks to other issues, but when they discussed the top five issues (except for the fifth, which was completely ignored), the frequency of mention corresponded to the importance of that issue to voters.

DISCUSSION

In this section, the functions, topics, forms of policy and character, targets of attacks, and issues addressed by the candidates in these 1992 debates will be discussed.

Functions of the 1992 Democratic Debates

Overall, more than twice as many themes enacted acclaims (65%) as attacks (32%). While the precise percentages varied somewhat from candidate to candidate, the basic relationship between acclaims and attacks held true for each individual candidate in these debates as well. This relationship is consistent with previous research on general presidential debates (Benoit, Blaney, & Pier, 1998; Benoit & Brazeal, in press; Benoit & Harthcock, 1999b; Wells, 2000). Both acclaims and attacks have the potential to improve one's net preferability. Acclaims (if persuasive) can increase one's favorability, whereas attacks can reduce an opponent's favorability (which yields a net increase in the attacking candidate's preferability). However, voters profess to dislike mudslinging (Merritt, 1984; Stewart, 1975). Thus, attacks have a greater possibility of producing a backlash. It makes perfect sense for acclaims to be more frequent than attacks in these primary debates.

We also found that defenses were relatively uncommon (3%), and the percentage of utterances that fell into this category was the smallest function for each candidate. Once again, this is consistent with past work investigating debates from the general campaign (Benoit, Blaney, & Pier, 1998; Benoit & Brazeal, in press; Benoit & Harthcock, 1999b; Wells, 2000). Defenses have even more potential drawbacks than attacks. First, they take the candidate "off-message," addressing an issue that probably favors an opponent. Second, defenses can create the impression that a candidates is reactive rather than proactive (appearing, as it were, "defensive"). Third, one cannot defend against an attack without identifying the criticism. Mentioning an attack, to allow a defense against that charge, could have the unintended effect of informing or reminding voters of an alleged weakness. While some attacks need a response, at other times it might be just as well to leave the matter alone. Thus, there are several reasons to expect that defenses would be far less common than either acclaims or attacks.

Topics of the 1992 Democratic Debates

Overall, more than twice as many utterances in these debates addressed policy (68%) as character (32%). Each of the candidates in these debates devoted more of their comments to policy than character. This finding mirrors results of past studies of general debates (Benoit, Blaney, & Pier, 1998; Benoit & Brazeal, in press; Benoit & Harthcock, 1999b; Wells, 2000). It is possible that there is some "spillover" from policy to character or from character to policy. For example, a candidate who frequently acclaims goals or programs to help the poor and disadvantaged (policy) may be seen as being more compassionate. At times candidates attack an opponent's inconsistent position on an issue (policy), but these conflicting policy positions can foster the impression that this candidate should not be trusted. On the other hand, a candidate who frequently boasts of compassion might be assumed to hold a certain issue position on social issues. A candidate who acclaims his record as a war hero (character) could easily be assumed to favor a strong defense (policy). Nevertheless, when these candidates spoke in these debates, there was a clear and consistent emphasis on policy over character.

Policy utterances were divided fairly evenly between future plans (38%) and general goals (35%). There were fewer past deeds (26%). This division of policy remarks could reflect the fact that there is no incumbent among these debaters. While each had held office (as senator or governor), no one had been in the White House. This may explain why, when they did discuss past deeds, they were far more likely to attack (184 times) than to acclaim (38 times).

Ideals were the most common form of character utterance (64%). Talk about personal qualities was only slightly more common (20%) than discussion of leadership ability (16%) in these debates. Again, it is possible that the fact that these were challengers, who wanted to chart a new direction for the federal government, away from President Bush's conservatism, could account for this emphasis.

We note in passing that the candidates were more likely to acclaim than attack both general goals (268 acclaims; 30 attacks) and ideals (182 acclaims; 76 attacks). General policy positions (strengthen the economy, reduce taxes, build a strong defense) and values (freedom, opportunity, choice) are much easier to praise than criticize.

Target of Attack in the 1992 Democratic Debates

Together these candidates attacked the status quo (59%) and the Republicans (19%) more than they attacked one another (22%). This does run counter to our expectations, because we would have expected more attacks against their immediate opponents (each other) than we observed. However, these candidates did not attack Bush and the Republicans more than they attacked each other; they directed most of their ire toward the establishment that they proposed to change.

Issues Addressed in the 1992 Democratic Debates

The largest category of the candidates' remarks falls into the classification "other." This means that they did not spend most of their time talking about the issues that were most important to voters. However, when they did talk about the top five issues, the rank order of their comments mirrored the rank of an issue in the polls. That is, they devoted more comments (34%) to the top issue, the economy; followed by the second issue, health care (12%); then jobs (9%), the third issue; and education, the fourth most important issue to the public (3%). None of the comments in these debates addressed the issue that was fifth most important to voters—poverty/homelessness.

CONCLUSION

The 1992 Democratic primary debates set the stage for the general election. Tsongas, Harkin, and Kerrey dropped out by mid-March. Brown remained in the race, but his presence was a reminder that the government has some grand problems that must be corrected. Ultimately, Bill Clinton won the right to face, and defeat, President George Bush in the 1992 general election.

8

2000: Who Will Be the First President of the New Millennium?

In the 2000 primary debates Bill Clinton was finishing his second term in office, and the vice president, Al Gore, wanted to succeed him. The economy was in good shape, and the federal government was producing surpluses, which the next president would have to present a plan for using (some combination of tax cuts, debt reduction, or increases in government spending). The 2000 primary campaign provided an opportunity to watch and analyze a number of debates by both parties. This chapter will present the results of our analysis of 3 Republican and 3 Democratic debates. We analyze a sample of the 22 debates that were held during the 2000 primaries. In this chapter the 2000 Republican debates will be analyzed, followed by a discussion of the 2000 Democratic debates. Finally, we will compare the Republican and Democratic debates.

2000 REPUBLICAN DEBATES

The analysis of the Republican debates will begin with a discussion of the background and context of the 2000 Republican primary. Second, the functions of the debates will be reported. This is followed by the analysis of topics and targets of attacks found in the Republican debates. Finally, the issues addressed in the 2000 Republican debates will be discussed.

Background of the 2000 Republican Debates

Republicans were faced with many choices for their presidential nominee in the 2000 primary. Pat Buchanan, who had contested the

Republican nomination in 1992 and 1996, announced his candidacy on March 2, 1999. He switched to the Reform Party and later became that party's nominee. Elizabeth Dole and Dan Quayle ran but dropped out before the debates. Gary Bauer, George W. Bush, Steve Forbes, Orrin Hatch, Alan Keyes, and John McCain participated in at least some of the 2000 Republican primary debates. The first debate, on October 22, 1999, in New Hampshire, included Bauer, Forbes, Hatch, Keyes, and McCain (but not Bush, the front-runner). The final debate took place on March 2, 2000, in California. Bush, Keyes, and McCain participated in that encounter.

The three Republican debates chosen for analysis took place on October 22, 1999, in Durham, New Hampshire (10/22/99, NH); November 21, 1999, in Tempe, Arizona (11/21/99, AZ); and February 15, 2000, in Columbia, South Carolina (2/15/00, SC). The October 22, 1999, debate included Gary Bauer, Steve Forbes, Orrin Hatch, Alan Keyes, and John McCain. Republicans Steve Forbes, Orrin Hatch, Alan Keyes, and John McCain met in Arizona on November 21, 1999. The final Republican debate in our analysis featured George W. Bush, Alan Keyes, and John McCain. Both Forbes and Keyes had run unsuccessfully in 1996 when Dole secured the Republican nomination but lost to Clinton/Gore. George W. Bush's father, President George H. W. Bush, lost his 1992 reelection bid to the team of Clinton/Gore. Results from all three Republican debates were combined for the analyses reported here.

Functions of the 2000 Republican Debates

For the Republicans, acclaims (66%) were the most common function in the debates. For example, Forbes acclaimed the following future plan in New Hampshire: "Under my plan, not only will there be substantial tax cuts, but in the next 10 years of this century, wages will up 60%" (10/22/99, NH). Forbes' plans for future tax cuts and increased wages would seem desirable to many Republican voters, so this utterance is an acclaim. Another example of acclaiming can be found in the Arizona debate from Hatch: "I'd let the Russians know that there'll be a lot of discontinuation of monetary help to Russia" (11/21/99, AZ). In this statement Hatch praises his general goals for foreign policy. In sum, acclaims were the most common function among the Republican debaters. Not only were acclaims most common collectively, but acclaims predominated for each individual Republican. See Table 8.1.

Attacks were the second most common function (30%). In South Carolina, for example, McCain attacked Bush's campaign tactics when he said: "But you're putting out stuff that is unbelievable, George, and it's got to stop" (2/15/00, SC). In this statement McCain attacks Bush's personal qualities by insinuating that Bush is disseminating informa-

TABLE 8.1
Functions of the 2000 Republican Debates

	Acclaims	Attacks	Defenses
Bauer	33 (58%)	24 (42%)	0
Bush	159 (72%)	40 (18%)	23 (10%)
Forbes	102 (66%)	52 (34%)	1 (1%)
Hatch	99 (82%)	22 (18%)	0
Keyes	175 (58%)	123 (41%)	3 (1%)
McCain	190 (66%)	86 (30%)	10 (4%)
Total	758 (66%)	347 (30%)	37 (4%)

tion about McCain and his campaign that is not believable. Bush responded by accusing McCain of the same tactic when he declared: "You can disagree with me on issues, John, but do not question—do not question my trustworthiness and do not compare me to Bill Clinton" (2/15/00, SC). In addition to acclaims, attacks were another frequent function of the Republican primary debates.

Defenses were the least common function of the Republican primary debates (4%). An example of a defense can be found in the South Carolina debate when Bush and McCain were arguing about less-than-honorable statements made by members of their campaign staffs. McCain attacked Bush's lack of effort to repudiate an attack made against McCain by a Bush staff member. Bush defended himself by stating: "I stood up there at that press conference and said, John, you're a man who served our country well" (2/15/00, SC). In this instance, Bush attempted to defend his personal character and integrity by rejecting the allegation that he failed to defend McCain's patriotism. While uncommon, defenses did occur in the 2000 Republican primary debates.

Topics of the 2000 Republican Debates

During the primary debates, Republicans discussed policy (55%) roughly as often as character (45%). For example, Keyes acclaimed his future plans (policy) for the tax system in this country when he declared: "The key to making sure we're able to take advantage of the enormous opportunities our technology is handing us, is to get back control of our money by abolishing the income tax" (10/22/99, NH). Clearly Keyes is appealing to voters' concerns about the current tax system, a policy matter. However, acclaiming character is also an option for candidates to garner support from the constituency. For example, in South Carolina Bush discussed his approach to campaign finance disclosure when he stated: "I want you to know who's given [to our campaign] because I don't want to hide anything" (2/15/00, SC). In this statement, although Bush refers to a policy topic that was discussed earlier (campaign finance reform) the primary purpose of the statement is to show that Bush is honest, a character consideration. In short, both policy and character were topics of discussion for the Republicans in the primary debates. See Table 8.2.

The Republican candidates devoted the largest percentage of their policy utterances to general goals (49%). For example, Keyes argued, "I think it's very important that we send a strong and unequivocal message to the Russian government that we are not going to tolerate idly the abuses that are taking place in Chechnya" (11/21/99 AZ). Keyes offers a general goal of "sending a message" to Russia to curb abuses of power taking place in that country. However, Keyes does not specifically outline what that "message" would entail, which makes this utterance a general goal (an end) rather than a future plan (a means to an end). The remaining policy utterances were distributed fairly evenly between past deeds (29%) and future plans (22%). Keyes attacked past deeds (joining the World Trade Organization [WTO]) when he stated, "I think we gave away a portion of our sovereignty that we should never have surrendered to an unrepresentative body that can make decisions according to that treaty that would have direct affect on the lives of Americans" (2/15/00, SC). In this excerpt Keyes criticized the establishment for entering into the WTO. Bauer acclaimed his future plans when he claimed, "And so my plan pays those IOUs to our parents and grandparents, but it also allows younger workers to have a 20-percent tax cut that they can invest anywhere" (10/22/99, NH). Here Bauer refers to his plans to improve the Social Security system.

Character utterances were divided somewhat evenly between personal qualities (43%) and ideals (47%). An example of an utterance concerning personal qualities is seen in a statement by Hatch, who said, "That's why I've been talking about having a common sense president

TABLE 8.2
Topics of the 2000 Republican Debates

	Policy	Character
Bauer	36 (63%)	21 (37%)
Bush	112 (56%)	87 (44%)
Forbes	103 (67%)	51 (33%)
Hatch	69 (57%)	52 (43%)
Keyes	128 (43%)	170 (57%)
McCain	160 (58%)	116 (42%)
Total	608 (55%)	497 (45%)

who literally will set an example, morally, from an integrity standpoint" (10/22/99, NH). In this excerpt Hatch implies that his personal qualities of morality and integrity are important in a president. Keyes provided an example of ideals when he stated, "We have got a country that has abandoned its most profound and fundamental principle. Killing babies in the womb every day is a contradiction" (2/15/00, SC). Here Keyes clearly indicates that one of his ideals, or values, is that of preserving life. Leadership ability (10%) received the least attention by the Republicans. For example, Hatch raised the question of future nominations for the Supreme Court: "And the only one running for president this year who's had a lot of experience in that area happens to be me" (11/21/99, AZ). In this excerpt Hatch was arguing that he had the most experience in appointing (or giving advice and consent for) Supreme Court judges, an issue that is important to the 2000 election. See Table 8.3.

Target of Attack in the 2000 Republican Debates

A majority of the attacks (55%) were targeted toward other Republican opponents. When these Republicans attacked members of their own party, the most frequent target was Bush (46%). For example, Keyes attacked Bush for his negative campaigning when he said, "I frankly believe that you spend all this time beating up on somebody else because you don't have that much to say yourself" (2/15/00, SC). Bush was the presumed front-runner, therefore drawing the majority of attention during the debates. McCain was also a popular target of attack (35%) for fellow Republican contenders. For example, Hatch attacked McCain's campaign reform plans as detrimental to the Republican Party when he stated, "Give me a break! If McCain-

TABLE 8.3
Forms of Policy and Character in the 2000 Republican Debates

	Policy						Character					
	Past Deeds*		Future Plans		General Goals		Personal Qualities		Leadership Ability		Ideals	
Bauer	1	10	7	4	13	1	1	8	1	0	10	1
Bush	10	14	20	2	60	6	18	16	22	1	29	1
Forbes	5	31	28	2	33	4	0	8	0	4	36	3
Hatch	22	13	6	0	24	4	8	3	5	0	34	2
Keyes	1	28	15	10	57	17	19	64	6	0	77	4
McCain	16	27	32	9	69	7	29	40	7	1	37	2
Total	55	123	108	27	256	39	75	139	41	6	223	13
	178		135		295		214		47		236	
	(29%)		(22%)		(49%)		(43%)		(10%)		(47%)	

*Acclaims/attacks.

Feingold passed, we basically would not have a Republican Party two years later, I guarantee you" (11/21/99, AZ). Although attacked less frequently than Bush, McCain was ranked second among Republican contenders in public opinion polls, thereby eliciting several attacks. In addition, both Bush and McCain held political offices at the time of the debate, making their past records fodder for the other contenders. Keyes (7%), Bauer (2%), Forbes (3%), and Hatch (2%) were all attacked by their fellow Republicans. However, they were attacked less frequently than Bush or McCain. Some utterances occasionally attacked the Republican Party generally (5%).

The status quo (21%) was a frequent target in the Republican primary debates. Forbes (who has not held elective office) provided an example of an attack against the establishment when he accused Washington bureaucrats of robbing constituents of their autonomy when it comes to making health care decisions: "The Washington top-down approach won't work. Giving people control of those resources will" (10/22/99, NH). During the primary campaign some candidates wish to portray themselves as "Washington outsiders" not jaded or corrupted by the political machine. Attacking the establishment becomes a way for such candidates to distinguish themselves from the "career politicians." This seems to be dictated by the candidate's situation: Those with records in office acclaim their experience and attack their opponents as untested; those without governmental experience tout their status as outsiders and attack others as career bureaucrats.

The Democrats (including Vice President Gore and President Clinton) received 24% of the attacks in the Republican primary debates. Hatch attacked both Gore and Clinton when he accused them of being less than sincere in their commitment to public education: "Keep in mind Al Gore and President Clinton love public education so much that they sent all their children to private schools" (10/22/99, NH). As the assumed leader of the opposition party, Gore would naturally sustain attacks from the Republicans. Although the primary functions to select one Republican from a field of many, it can also serve to distinguish one party from another. Gore served as Clinton's vice president for eight years, so Republicans in the primaries attacked Gore by associating him with President Clinton, who was not particularly popular among Republican voters. See Table 8.4.

Issues Addressed in the 2000 Republican Debates

Republican candidates in these debates devoted most of their policy remarks to topics other than the issues that were most important to voters. Fully 74% of their comments addressed other topics besides the top five issues of Social Security, the economy, education, morals, and

TABLE 8.4
Target of Attack in the 2000 Republican Debates

	Own Party (Republicans)							Dems.	Establishment
	Bauer	*Bush*	*Forbes*	*Hatch*	*Keyes*	*McCain*	*Reps.*		
Bauer	—	1	3	0	0	1	1	7	11
Bush	0	—	0	0	3	19	0	9	9
Forbes	0	13	—	1	0	0	2	19	17
Hatch	1	0	0	—	1	4	2	10	4
Keyes	2	40	2	2	—	43	0	20	14
McCain	0	34	0	0	10	—	5	20	17
Total	3	88	5	3	14	67	10	85	72
	(2%)	(46%)	(3%)	(2%)	(7%)	(35%)	(5%)	(24%)	(21%)
				190 (55%)					

health care. At times, though, the Republican candidates did discuss the issues that were most important to voters. For example, the top issue for voters was Social Security, and McCain praised his future plans for Social Security when he said, "You take 62 percent of the surplus and you put it into Social Security to make it solvent. Then you take the Congress and tell them to keep their hands off it" (11/21/99, AZ). The second most important issue was the economy. Keyes promised that if elected, he would "restore control of our money and our economy to the people" (11/21/99, AZ). Voters ranked education as the third most important issue. In New Hampshire, McCain discussed the importance of "choice and competition in education" (10/22/99, NH). The fifth issue for voters was health care. Forbes offered an attack of Bush's lack of health care plans: "Again, on health care, George Bush has put nothing on the table, just vague ideas, nothing real" (11/21/99, AZ). These excerpts illustrate how the Republicans discussed the various policy topics. See Table 8.5.

TABLE 8.5
Issues Addressed in the 2000 Republican Debates

	Social Security (17%)	Economy (16%)	Education (15%)	Morals (13%)	Health Care (12%)	Other (27%)
Bauer	3	0	8	0	5	20
Bush	2	1	5	0	3	102
Forbes	5	2	18	0	15	63
Hatch	1	0	8	0	12	48
Keyes	1	0	14	0	7	106
McCain	11	2	17	0	12	100
Total	23	5	70	0	54	439
	(4%)	(1%)	(12%)		(9%)	(74%)

2000 DEMOCRATIC DEBATES

The discussion of Democratic debates begins with a review of the background and context of the 2000 Democratic primary. This will be followed by a report of the functions of the debates, the topics of these encounters, and targets of attacks in the Democratic debates. Finally, the issues addressed in the three 2000 Democratic debates we analyzed will be covered.

Background of the 2000 Democratic Debates

Gore's quest for the Democratic nomination was challenged by former Senator Bill Bradley, who announced his candidacy on December 4, 1998. Bill Bradley, who had been an NBA star and a senator, was Gore's only challenger. All told, Bradley and Gore engaged in nine debates from October 27, 1999, in New Hampshire through March 1, 2000 in California. The three Democratic debates chosen for analysis here took place on October 27, 1999, in Hanover, New Hampshire (10/27/99, NH); February 21, 2000, in New York City (2/21/00, NY); and March 1, 2000, in Los Angeles (3/1/00, CA). Gore was the current vice president, having served two terms with President Clinton, and was seeking to follow in George Bush's footsteps (Bush was Reagan's vice president for two terms, 1980 and 1984, and successfully ran for president in 1988). Results from all three Democratic debates were combined to produce the results reported here.

Functions of the 2000 Democratic Debates

The most common function in the Democratic debates was acclaiming (78%). For example, in the California debate Gore praised his approach to appointing Supreme Court justices when he said, "I would look for justices of the Supreme Court who understand that our Constitution is a living and breathing document, that it was intended by our founders to be interpreted in the light of the constantly evolving experience of the American people" (3/1/00, CA). Bradley acclaimed a future plan when he declared in New York that if elected "I would issue an executive order that would eliminate racial profiling at the federal level" (2/21/00, NY). He obviously expected that elimination of racial profiling was a proposal that would resonate with his audience. Acclaims were the most common function for Bradley and Gore individually as well as collectively. See Table 8.6.

Attacks (17%) were the second most common function of the Democratic debates. In the New Hampshire debate Bradley attacked the establishment for not adequately funding education: "Well, I think that

TABLE 8.6
Functions of the 2000 Democratic Debates

	Acclaims	Attacks	Defenses
Bradley	253 (76%)	63 (19%)	16 (5%)
Gore	294 (80%)	55 (15%)	20 (5%)
Total	547 (78%)	118 (17%)	36 (5%)

the federal government made a solemn commitment to fund up to 40 percent of special education. It's not doing that now at all" (10/27/99, NH). This indictment seemed aimed at both the Clinton/Gore administration and Congress. Gore attacked Republican candidates Bauer and Bush when he declared, "Both are in the hip pocket of the NRA [National Rifle Association]" (3/1/00, CA). Many of those who would be voting in Democratic primaries might tend to oppose the NRA. Thus, in addition to acclaiming, attacks were also used in the Democratic debates.

Defenses were the least common function of the Democratic primary debates (5%). An example of a defense is provided by Gore when he confessed his mistake in exaggerating his role in creating the Internet: "You know, I'm not proud of what I did to try to take too much credit for it" (10/27/99, NH). In New York, Bradley attacked Gore by declaring that the vice president "proposes increasing defense expenditures more than he proposes increasing education expenditures." The vice president responded to this accusation by asserting, "That's not true either, not true. That's not true either" (2/21/00, NY). This functions as a clear denial of Bradley's accusation. While not common, defenses did occur in the 2000 Democratic primary debates.

Topics of the 2000 Democratic Debates

Throughout the debates, Democrats discussed policy (70%) more than character (30%). For example, Bradley discussed policy when he praised his health care plan: "So I am glad that you've looked at the proposal and you see that it covers all children, that it brings many adults who don't have health coverage into the system now, that it provides a drug benefit for the elderly" (10/27/99, NH). In contrast, character was a topic of the Los Angeles debate when Bradley declared, "That's how I run this campaign. I believe the new politics is a politics of belief and conviction, of honestly telling people the truth" (3/1/00, CA). Clearly, honesty is a desirable quality for a candidate (and a president) to possess. In sum, both policy and character were topics of discussion for Democrats in the primary debates. However, each candidate focused primarily on policy. See Table 8.7.

General goals (54%) were the most common form of policy employed by the Democrats. For example, Bradley outlined a general approach to increasing oil prices when he stated, "But more importantly, we need to go to Kuwait and Saudi Arabia, those countries that we defended in the Gulf War, and we need to tell them to increase their oil production" (3/1/00, CA). No particular mechanism for increasing oil protection was referenced, so this is a general goal rather than a future plan. Past deeds (38%) were also commonly discussed by the Democratic candidates. Gore praised his past efforts for creating jobs and reducing poverty when he reported that "we have created in the last seven years 20 million new jobs in America and the lowest African-American unemployment rate and poverty rate in history" (2/21/00, NY). Finally, future plans (8%) was the least common form of policy used by Democratic candidates. Bradley outlined his plans for campaign finance reform when he said, "We both have ideas of what should happen: no soft money, public financing of elections, free TV time for people in the last six weeks of an election" (10/27/99, NH). In this excerpt Bradley clearly articulated the future policies (means) for achieving campaign finance reform that he would enact if elected.

Personal qualities (52%) were the most common form of character. Gore praised his personal qualities when he explained that "I have embarked on a career that is very demanding of a lot of hard work and commitment" (3/1/00, CA). Here Gore claims that he possesses personal qualities, specifically his work ethic and commitment. Ideals were mentioned approximately a third of the time (34%). In the same debate, Bradley revealed his ideals and values when he declared, "I think that there should be freedom of religion" (3/1/00, CA). Leadership ability (14%) received the least amount of attention by Democrats. For example, Gore discussed the leadership abilities that it takes to pass a comprehensive test ban treaty: "That will take a leadership that is able to engender trust on both sides of the aisle. It will take a leadership that makes the case farsighted enough and works with the Congress well enough to make it happen" (10/27/99, NH). In this statement Gore discusses the importance of strong

TABLE 8.7
Topics of the 2000 Democratic Debates

	Policy	Character
Bradley	213 (64%)	103 (36%)
Gore	251 (72%)	98 (28%)
Total	464 (70%)	201 (30%)

leadership in foreign policy and implies that he has what it takes to be effective. See Table 8.8.

Target of Attack in the 2000 Democratic Debates

The Democrats had several targets for their attacks. Most often Bradley and Gore would attack their immediate opponent (one another; 52%). An example of an attack can be found in Gore's criticism of Bradley's health care plan: "The respected Emory School of Public Health came out with a nonpartisan analysis of both my plan and Senator Bradley's and they said that his plan costs $1.2 trillion. That is more than the entire surplus over the next ten years" (10/27/99, NH). Obviously this is meant as a criticism of Bradley's proposal. Because there were only two participants in the Democratic debates, the situation was conducive to a sparring match between the two candidates.

The Republican Party (18%) was also attacked fairly often by Bradley and Gore. For example, Gore attacked the Republican front-runners when he declared, "Both Governor Bush and Senator McCain are as anti-choice as you can get" (3/1/00, CA). In the primary it is necessary to remind the constituents that although one must choose between the two candidates at hand, either choice is preferable to the opposing party. However, both candidates attacked their own party (16%) as well. Both Bradley and Gore held political offices, and their records (and the record of their party) could be used against them. Often in the primary phase contenders seek to set themselves as something other than "a Washington politician" or more of the same old politics. Therefore, occasional attacks by Gore and Bradley on their own party may have helped to set them apart as "fresh" or unique (clearly Gore was trying to distance himself from Clinton in later stages of the campaign). Finally, both candidates attacked the status quo (14%). However, Bradley attacked the establishment far more often than Gore. Perhaps Brad-

TABLE 8.8
Forms of Policy and Character in the 2000 Democratic Debates

	Policy						Character				
	Past Deeds*		Future Plans		General Goals		Personal Qualities		Leadership Ability		Ideals	
Bradley	34	49	16	1	109	4	49	6	9	1	36	2
Gore	74	19	9	10	128	13	37	14	18	1	29	—
Total	108	68	25	11	237	17	86	20	27	2	65	2
	176 (38%)		36 (8%)		254 54%)		106 (52%)		29 (14%)		67 (33%)	

*Acclaims/attacks.

ley was trying to paint himself as less of a "Washington insider" than Gore by attacking the establishment. This may have created some contrast to Gore, a sitting vice president. See Table 8.9.

Issues Addressed in the 2000 Democratic Debates

Most often in these debates (69%), when candidates addressed policy, they talked about topics other than the top five issues. Social Security, which was the most important issue for voters, accounted for only 5% of Bradley's and Gore's remarks. For example, Gore declared, "What we need to do instead is to use the surplus to safeguard Social Security, first and foremost. I'm opposed to raising the retirement age or cutting Social Security benefits" (3/1/00, NY). The second most important issue in the poll data was the economy, which accounted for a mere 1% of the candidates' utterances. For instance, in New Hampshire, Bradley explained that if "you care about managing the economy so the growth takes more and more people to higher economic ground, then I would hope you'd feel that I would be your candidate" (10/27/99, NH). It seems particularly odd that Gore, as the sitting vice president, did not acclaim the current healthy economy more often than he did. Education, which was ranked third by voters, received more attention in these debates (12%). For example, Bradley praised his goals for education when he said, "I think that the national government should increase what it spends on special ed, thereby liberating monies that are raised locally to be spent locally on general school needs" (10/27/99, NH). Morals, ranked the fourth most important issue by the public, was addressed in 7% of the policy themes in these debates. For example, Bradley discussed morals when he responded to an inquiry from Reverend Sharpton about racial profiling: "Reverend Sharpton, when I think of Amadou Diallo, I think of an unarmed man who was fired at 41 times by the police, who was killed. I think it was an outrage" (2/21/00, NY). Finally, health care, ranked fifth by voters, received 6% of the Democratic policy utterances. In the same debate Gore discussed

TABLE 8.9
Target of Attack in the 2000 Democratic Debates

	Own Party		Republicans	Establishment
	Opponent	Other Democrats		
Bradley	26	9	10	14
Gore	33	9	11	2
Total	59	18	21	16
	77 (68%)		(18%)	(14%)

the topic of health care when he stated, "Well, I'm in favor of the so-called catastrophic protection, and we put money in the budget this year to take care of that" (2/21/00, CA). Thus, the candidates did not address the bulk of their remarks to the issues that were most important to voters. See Table 8.10.

PARTY COMPARISONS

This section provides a brief comparison between the Democratic and Republican primary debates in the 2000 campaign. The functions, topics, targets of attacks, and issues addressed in these debates will be discussed.

Functions of the 2000 Debates

Analysis of the data reveals that the two political parties differed significantly in their use of functions in these debates. A chi-square calculated on differences between the Republicans and Democrats in use of functions was significant (χ^2[df = 2] = 43.9, p <.001). Although both Republicans (66%, 30%, and 4%) and Democrats (78%, 17%, 5%) acclaim more than attack and attack more than they defend, these Republicans attacked more, and acclaimed less, than these Democrats. This may be due to the fact that there were more contenders for the Republican nomination, thereby making it more important for the candidates to highlight their differences from the others. See Table 8.11.

Topics of the 2000 Debates

A chi-square also indicated that there were significant differences between the parties in their use of policy and character utterances (χ^2[df = 1] = 37.8, p < .001). Republicans had a modest preference for policy over character (55%, 45%). Democrats, on the other hand, utilized policy considerations (70%) over twice as much as character (30%). Perhaps the Republicans' antipathy toward Clinton led them to stress

TABLE 8.10
Issues Addressed in the 2000 Democratic Debates

	Social Security (17%)	Economy (16%)	Education (15%)	Morals (13%)	Health Care (12%)	Other
Bradley	10	1	28	14	13	149
Gore	15	1	26	17	17	175
Total	25 (5%)	2 (1%)	54 (12%)	31 (7%)	30 (6%)	324 (69%)

TABLE 8.11
Functions of the 2000 Democratic vs. Republican Debates

	Acclaims	Attacks	Defenses
Democrats	547 (78%)	118 (17%)	36 (5%)
Republicans	758 (66%)	347 (30%)	37 (4%)

character more than Democrats, or led the Democrats to avoid this topic. See Table 8.12.

There was a difference between the parties in the forms of policy they used (χ^2[df = 2] = 42.4, p < .001). Democrats concentrated on past deeds (38%) to a greater extent than Republicans (29%). This could be because both Democratic candidates had previous experience in office (Bradley was a senator, and Gore has served in Congress and as the vice president), whereas several of the Republican candidates (Bauer, Forbes, and Keyes) had no, or minimal, government experience. Given the fact that, as a group, Republicans could not acclaim on past deeds as often as the Democratic debaters, their policy utterances had to address either future plans or general goals more frequently. Republicans offered future plans (22%) far more often than Democrats (8%). A greater emphasis on future plans by Republicans could stem from the fact that the Democratic Party held the White House. Although the incumbent party can, and does, use future plans, this is a more common strategy with challengers. After all, one proposes a future plan to correct a problem, and the challengers have more of an incentive to decry the present state of affairs than the incumbents. Democrats discussed general goals (54%) at roughly the same level as the Republicans (49%).

A chi-square revealed a significant difference between the parties in the forms of character (χ^2[df = 2] = 12.7, p < .01). While both parties addressed leadership ability the least, the Democratic candidates addressed their personal qualities (52%) much more often than their ideals (34%). Republicans were somewhat equal in their use of personal qualities (43%) and ideals (47%). It is possible that the Democratic candidates were sensitive to the criticisms of character that surrounded Bill Clinton's presidency and were preempting possible attacks by Republican candidates. As for the Republicans, since there were a greater number of participants and a greater variety of ideals represented, it is

TABLE 8.12
Topics of the 2000 Democratic vs. Republican Debates

	Policy	Character
Democrats	464 (70%)	201 (30%)
Republicans	608 (55%)	497 (45%)

plausible that the candidates had to distinguish themselves at both personal and ideological levels. See Table 8.13.

Target of Attack in the 2000 Debates

The Republicans devoted more of their attacks to their immediate opponents, members of their own party, than did the Democrats (Republicans: 68%; Democrats, 55%). Conversely, the Democrats in these debates attacked the opposing party more than the Republicans did (Democrats: 25%; Republicans: 18%). Democrats also tended to attack the status quo a bit more than Republicans (Democrats: 21%; Republicans: 14%). However, a chi-square revealed that these differences were not statistically significant (χ^2[df = 2] = 5.9, n.s.). See Table 8.14.

Issues Addressed in the 2000 Debates

Candidates in both parties focused more time on other issues than the topics that were most important to voters (Republicans: 74%; Democrats: 69%). Both parties apportioned most of their comments (12% each) to the third most important issue, education. Next was the fifth issue to voters, health care (Republicans: 9%; Democrats: 6%). Despite the Republican moral crusade against Bill Clinton—or perhaps indeed because of it—the Democrats addressed moral issues more than the Republicans. The most important issue to voters, Social Security, received a mere 5% of the Democratic policy utterances and 4% from the Republicans. The second most important issue according to the polls, the economy, was addressed in only 1% of the comments by each party. See Table 8.15.

Thus, the parallels between the two parties on issues addressed are remarkable. Neither appears to be effectively engaging in audience analysis. Of course, the questions asked in these debates influence the candidates' utterances. However, in opening and closing statements the

TABLE 8.13

Forms of Policy and Character in the 2000 Democratic vs. Republican

	Policy						Character					
	Past Deeds*		Future Plans		General Goals		Personal Qualities		Leadership Ability		Ideals	
Democrats	108	68	25	11	237	17	86	20	27	2	65	2
	176		36		254		106		29		67	
	(38%)		(8%)		(54%)		(52%)		(14%)		(33%)	
Republicans	55	123	108	27	256	39	75	139	41	6	223	13
	178		125		295		214		47		236	
	(29%)		(22%)		(49%)		(43%)		(10%)		(47%)	

*Acclaims/attacks.

The Primary Decision

TABLE 8.14
Target of Attack in the 2000 Democratic vs. Republican Debates

	Own Party	Other Party	Establishment
Democrats	77 (68%)	21 (18%)	16 (14%)
Republicans	190 (55%)	85 (24%)	72 (21%)

candidates can select their own topics. They can also switch from the topic of the question to another topic in midstatement. Failure to focus most comments on the topics that are most important to voters cannot be blamed entirely on the questioners.

CONCLUSION

Analysis of the 2000 Republican and Democratic debates revealed how they used the functions and topics of campaign discourse in these messages. Republicans attacked more than Democrats, possibly because of the larger number of candidates. Both parties focused more on policy than character. However, the Democrats focused even more on policy than the Republicans, while the Republicans emphasized character more than the Democrats. Perhaps this Republican emphasis on character is a residual effect from the impeachment and trial of President Bill Clinton. Democrats focused more on past deeds than Republicans, perhaps because fewer Republicans in the debates had governmental experience. This, and the fact that the Republicans wanted to wrest control of the White House from the Democrats, could also account for greater use of future plans by the Republicans. The Republican contenders attacked one another a bit more than the Democrats, whereas the Democrats had a slight edge in attacks on the opposing party. These candidates did not focus their debate remarks on the issues that were most important to voters.

TABLE 8.15
Issues Addressed in the 2000 Democratic vs. Republican Debates

	Social Security (17%)	Economy (16%)	Education (15%)	Morals (13%)	Health Care (12%)	Other (27%)
Democrats	25 (5%)	2 (1%)	54 (12%)	31 (7%)	30 (6%)	324 (69%)
Republicans	23 (4%)	5 (1%)	70 (12%)	0	54 (9%)	439 (74%)

Princeton Survey Research Associates, 1999.

9

Conclusions

The data collected and analyzed for this study represents 25 primary debates from 10 campaigns (including 1996, reported in Benoit, Blaney & Pier, 1998). These debates included 47 different participants (several of these 47 candidates participated in multiple debates). A total of 26 different Republicans and 21 different Democrats clashed in these debates. Both candidates who won the primary and became their party's nominees (12—although Humphrey participated in a primary debate in 1960 but became the nominee in 1968) and candidates who lost the primary campaign (35) are represented in these data. Although there are other debates that we did not analyze, and these debates are a convenience sample (many debates were not available to us), we are confident that these data represent a substantial, broad, and diverse portion of the universe of presidential primary debates.

This chapter will examine each of the 17 hypotheses posed at the beginning of this study. The results for each hypothesis will be presented and then discussed. Because our research program has already investigated general debates and primary television spots, those message forms will be used as points of comparison in our analysis. Results will be grouped into three areas: results related to the Functional Theory of Political Campaign Discourse, results concerning primary campaigns, and results relevant to political debates. Finally, we will address the implications of these findings.

FUNCTIONAL THEORY OF POLITICAL CAMPAIGN DISCOURSE

We proposed four hypotheses that pertain to the Functional Theory of Political Campaign Discourse. One concerns the distribution of the three functions. A second addresses the distribution of topics. A third hypothesis concerns the relationship between attacks and defenses. The final hypothesis in this section addresses the distribution of acclaims and attacks on General Goals and Ideals.

Acclaims Outnumber Attacks, Which Outnumber Defenses

The first hypothesis (H1), concerning the distribution of the three functions of campaign discourse in primary debates, was confirmed. Acclaims accounted for 63% of the utterances in these primary debates. For example, in the New York City Apollo Theater debate of February 21, 2000, Bradley acclaimed this future plan: "I would issue an executive order that would eliminate racial profiling at the federal level." Attacks constituted 32% of the themes analyzed in these debates. In that same debate, Bradley chastised Gore for "his vote to preserve tax exempt status for schools like Bob Jones that racially discriminate." Finally, defenses accounted for 4% of the remarks by these candidates. Gore offered this response, denying Bradley's accusation that Gore had supported tax-exempt status for Bob Jones University: "Bob Jones University lost its tax exemption under the law that I supported. They still do not have a tax exemption. So, that is a phony and scurrilous charge." All three functions occurred in these primary debates.

A one-way chi-square confirms that these utterances are not distributed equally across the three functions ($\chi^2[df = 1] = 4281.8$, $p < .001$). These results are consistent with results of analysis of both general debates—acclaims (55%) > attacks (35%) > defenses (10%)—and results of research on primary television spots—acclaims (71%) > attacks (28%) > defenses (1%)—as Tables 9.1 and 9.2 reveal.

TABLE 9.1
Functions of Debates

	Acclaims	Attacks	Defenses
Primary	5,121 (63%)	2,593 (32%)	355 (4%)
General	2,532 (55%)	1,633 (35%)	442 (10%)
Total	7,653 (60%)	4,226 (33%)	797 (6%)

$\chi^2[df = 2] = 170.6$, $p < .001$.

TABLE 9.2
Functions of Primary Messages

	Acclaims	Attacks	Defenses
Debates	5,121 (63%)	2,593 (32%)	355 (4%)
TV Spots	3,409 (71%)	1,318 (28%)	53 (1%)
Total	8,530 (66%)	3,911 (30%)	408 (3%)

$\chi^2[df = 2] = 150.8$, $p < .001$.

Each of the three functions can help a candidate appear preferable to opponents. However, because voters report their distaste for attacks (Merritt, 1984; Stewart, 1975; although that does not necessarily prove attacks are ineffective), candidates have a reason to produce more acclaims than attacks. Furthermore, there are several reasons for candidates to engage in relatively few defenses. First, one can only refute an argument by acknowledging it. This means candidates run the risk of reminding or informing voters of attacks that could have been missed or forgotten when they identify an attack in order to defend against it. Second, most attacks presumably occur on issues that favor one's opponent. This means that responding to an attack can take a candidate "off message," and that means the defending candidate is spending time on issues that probably favor the attacking candidate. Third, using too many defenses could make a candidate appear to be on the defensive, responding rather than initiating. Still, some attacks cannot be ignored and do provoke defenses. Thus, we expected, and found, that defenses would occur, albeit less frequently than attacks or acclaims.

More Utterances Address Policy Than Character

The second hypothesis (H2) addressed the allocation of the two broad topics of campaign discourse, policy and character. Analysis of the data reveals that 63% of primary debate utterances concern policy, whereas 37% of themes addressed character, confirming this hypothesis. For example, in the South Carolina debate of January 7, 2000, Bush declared, "I would be a free-trading president, a president that will work tirelessly to open up markets for agricultural products all over the world." Clearly this goal concerns policy. Similarly, Forbes addressed tax policy when he explained in the same debate: "I want to get rid of this corrupt tax code, allow the American people to genuinely keep more of what they earn." However, at times the primary debaters also discussed character. For example, Keyes emphasized the critical nature of honesty in South Carolina: "I think that it's important, however, that we be honest and forthright." Bush identified a different quality in this utterance from the same debate: "I intend to rally the armies of compassion all across America should I become the president to help people in need with people in heart." Thus, these candidates addressed both policy and character in primary debates.

A one-way *chi-square* confirms that these utterances are not distributed equally across the three functions ($\chi^2[df = 1] = 452.9$, $p < .001$). These results are consistent with the distribution of topics in general debates (policy = 75%, character = 25%), as Table 9.3 demonstrates. The distribution of topics in primary television spots is more nearly equal (policy = 53%, character = 47%), with some tendency to emphasize policy. See Table 9.4.

While we would not argue that character is unimportant, for many people the primary job of the president is to run the executive branch of government, which involves domestic and foreign policy. Public opinion poll data from 1976 to 2000 (every year in which we could find the question posed in a public opinion poll) reveal that for most voters policy is a more important determinant of their presidential vote than character (Table 9.5). Thus, it appears that candidates are responding to voter preferences when they spend more time on policy than character in these presidential primary debates.

Attacks Are Positively Related to Defenses

For the next hypothesis (H3), we calculated the number of attacks on each candidate along with the number of defenses produced by that candidate. The Pearson's *r* for these data is .71 ($p < .001$, $N = 88$), showing that there is a significant positive relationship between the number of attacks directed toward candidates and the number of defenses generated by them. In fact, an *r* of .71 means that 50% of the variance in production of defenses can be explained by provoking attacks.

This relationship makes perfect sense. First, one cannot, by definition, produce a defense except in response to an attack. Therefore, a candidate has to be attacked before he or she can produce a meaningful

TABLE 9.3
Topics of Debates

	Policy	Character
Primary	4,865 (63%)	2,890 (37%)
General	2,705 (75%)	911 (25%)
Total	7,570 (67%)	3,801 (33%)

$\chi^2[df = 1] = 161.5$, $p < .001$.

TABLE 9.4
Topics of Primary Messages

	Policy	*Character*
Debates	4,865 (63%)	2,890 (37%)
TV Spots	2,053 (52%)	1,874 (48%)
Total	7,272 (59%)	5,046 (41%)

$\chi^2[df = 1] = 118.4$, $p < .001$.

defense. Second, as the number of attacks one faces increases, there are both more opportunities to defend and more motivation for the candidate who has been attacked to produce defenses. Thus, finding a significant positive correlation between number of provoking attacks and number of defenses confirmed our expectations about the relationship between these two functions.

More Acclaims Than Attacks on General Goals and Ideals

The next hypothesis (H4) addressed the allocation of acclaims and attacks on two specific topics, general goals and ideals. There are far more acclaims than attacks on general goals (1,682 to 270) and on ideals (1,105 to 214) (see Table 9.6). This same relationship has been found in other political messages as well as primary debates as Table 9.7 displays. In general debates, there were more acclaims than attacks on general goals (486; 96) as well as on ideals (284; 67; see Benoit, Blaney, & Pier, 1998; Benoit & Brazeal, in press; Benoit & Harthcock, 1999b; Wells, 2000). In primary television spots, there were 764 acclaims and 122 attacks on general goals; 340 acclaims and 36 attacks on ideals

TABLE 9.5
Most Important Determinant of Presidential Vote

Campaign	*Policy*	*Character*	*Poll*
1976	57%	36%	CBS/*New York Times*
1980	59%	34%	*LA Times*
1984	87%	7%	*LA Times*
1988	59%	16%	*USA Today*
1992	143%*	16%	Harris Poll
1996	65%	27%	NBC/*Wall Street Journal*
2000	90%	8%	Princeton Survey Research Associates 10/7-11/99

*Respondents were allowed to pick the two most important factors in this poll.
"Don't know" and "unsure" responses also occurred.
All polls obtained from Lexis/Nexis Academic Universe online.

TABLE 9.6
Forms of Policy and Character in Debates

	Policy			Character		
	Past Deeds*	Future Plans	General Goals	Personal Qualities	Leadership Ability	Ideals
Primary	571 | 1,252	774 | 389	1,682 | 270	624 | 432	435 | 115	1,105 | 214
	37%	24%	40%	36%	19%	45%
General	620 | 884	448 | 179	486 | 96	161 | 149	144 | 76	284 | 67
	55%	23%	21%	35%	25%	40%
Total	1,191 | 2,136	1,222 | 568	2,168 | 366	785 | 581	579 | 191	1389 | 281
	43%	23%	33%	36%	20%	44%

*Acclaims/attacks.

(Benoit, 1999). See Table 9.7. Even in general television spots (Benoit, 1999), acclaims also outnumbered attacks on general goals (642; 62) and on ideals (257; 48). Thus, there is a consistent tendency, occurring across message forms, for presidential candidates to acclaim more than they attack on general goals and ideals.

We believe that both goals and ideals are easier to acclaim than to attack. For example, it would be much easier to embrace than reject this goal articulated by Gore in the Apollo debate: "What we need to do . . . is to use the surplus to safeguard Social Security first and foremost." Who could disagree with the goal of safeguarding Social Security? Candidates might disagree about the best *means* for achieving this goal (future plans), but they are unlikely to attack the end itself. Similarly, Keyes articulated an ideal in the South Carolina debate that would be difficult to challenge: "We should be very careful not to become practitioners of aggression." It is easier to embrace goals than to develop specific policies to achieve those plans. Thus, it should not be surprising to find more acclaims than attacks on both general goals and ideals.

Therefore, data from our analysis of presidential primary debates confirm several tenets related to the Functional Theory of Political

TABLE 9.7
Forms of Policy and Character in Primary Messages

	Policy			Character		
	Past Deeds*	Future Plans	General Goals	Personal Qualities	Leadership Ability	Ideals
Debates	571 | 1,252	774 | 389	1,682 | 270	624 | 432	435 | 115	1,105 | 214
	37%	24%	40%	36%	19%	45%
TV Spots	396 | 498	348 | 141	968 | 141	760 | 371	480 | 125	424 | 39
	36%	20%	45%	51%	28%	21%
Total	967 | 1,750	1,122 | 530	2,650 | 411	1,384 | 803	915 | 240	1,529 | 253
	37%	22%	41%	43%	23%	35%

*Acclaims/attacks.

Campaign Discourse. Acclaims were more common than attacks, and attacks occurred more frequently than defenses. The candidates discussed policy more frequently than character. Third, attacks provoked (were positively related to) defenses. General goals and ideals were used more frequently to acclaim than to attack.

PRIMARY CAMPAIGNS

These debates occurred during the primary phase of the campaign. We believe that the campaign phase influences the messages produced by candidates. We advanced nine predictions about primary debates as messages developed for the primary campaign. Three of these hypotheses concern the functions of debates. Two pertain to the distribution of past deeds and general goals in the two campaign phases. Three address the target of attacks. Finally, one concerns the policy issues discussed by candidates.

Attacks Are Less Frequent in Primary Than General Debates

As predicted (H5), attacks were more common in general debates (35%) than in primary debates (32%). A chi-square calculated on functions and debates revealed a significant difference ($\chi^2[df = 2] = 170.6, p < .001$). See Table 9.1. This result is consistent with past research into television spots: Attacks made up 39% of the themes in general TV spots but only 31% of the themes in primary TV spots (Benoit, 1999).

It makes sense for candidates to moderate to some extent their attacks during the primary season. First, candidates will want their opponents in the primary season—and perhaps even more important, their opponents' adherents—to support them in the general campaign. For example, it is in George Bush's interests to avoid going overboard in his attacks on John McCain; if he alienates McCain or McCain's supporters by overly harsh primary attacks, they might not support him in the fall. (Still, Bush may feel compelled to attack McCain in order to secure the nomination.) But Bush has no similar reason to hold back from attacking Gore in the fall. (We note in passing that in the fall one of the authors of this book received recorded telephone messages from Elizabeth Dole and John McCain supporting Governor Bush.)

Second, candidates from one party will recycle attacks made in the primary against their fall opponents. For example, in 1964 Lyndon Johnson ran this television advertisement against Barry Goldwater:

Back in July in San Francisco, the Republicans held a convention. Remember him [Rockefeller poster]? He was there, Governor Rockefeller. Before the convention he said Barry Goldwater's positions can, and I quote, spell disaster for the party and for the country. Or him? Governor Scranton [Scranton poster]. The day before the convention, he called Goldwaterism a quote crazy quilt collection of absurd and dangerous positions. Or this man, Governor Romney [Romney poster]. In June he said Goldwater's nomination would lead to the quote suicidal destruction of the Republican Party. So, even if you are a Republican with serious doubts about Barry Goldwater, you're in good company [jumble of posters]. Vote for President Johnson on November 3. The stakes are too high for you to stay home. (Johnson, 1964)

Kendall (2000) argued that attacks made by Humphrey on McGovern were used by Nixon in the fall of 1972: "The [California primary] debates prove very damaging to McGovern. Not only did he plummet in the California polls, but Humphrey's vivid characterizations of McGovern's weaknesses provided rich material for Nixon in the fall campaign" (p. 78). Similarly, in the general election campaign in 2000, a television spot for Gore reminded voters, "In this year's election John McCain said Bush's plan has not provided one penny for social security." This was an attack McCain made in a television spot and in the January 15, 2000, Iowa primary debate. Thus, a second reason to moderate attacks in the primary is to avoid providing fodder for the other party's attacks in the general campaign.

A final reason to expect somewhat fewer attacks in the primary than in the general campaign is that, presumably, there are more grounds for attack in the fall (more differences between parties than within a party). While there were differences between Gore and Bradley in 2000 (and between the various Republican candidates), it seems likely that the differences between Gore and Bush will be greater. The more differences, the more opportunities for attack. Thus, we should expect, and we did find, that there would be fewer attacks in the primary than in the general campaign.

Defenses Are Less Frequent in Primary Than General Debates

As predicted (H6), defenses accounted for only 4% of the themes in primary debates but fully 10% of the themes in general debates. The fact that there are more attacks in general debates makes defenses more likely in that phase. Recall that hypothesis 3, discussed earlier, demonstrated that attacks are positively related to defenses. Benoit and Wells (1996) observed the following in the 1992 general debates:

We found a clear relationship between persuasive attack and persuasive defense. Examination of attack and defense by debate confirms this claim.

As the number of persuasive attacks dropped in the second debate, so did defensive utterances. . . . When the number of attacks increased in debate 3, persuasive defense increased as well. . . . We found that the most attacks (from Clinton and Perot) were aimed at Bush, who has the largest number of defenses utterances, and the fewest attacks were leveled (by either Bush or Clinton) at Perot, who presented the least number of defenses. (p. 112)

Thus, because there are more attacks in general debates, we should expect to find more defenses in that later campaign phase. See Table 9.1.

Acclaims Are More Frequent in Primary Than General Debates

As predicted (H7), acclaims accounted for 63% of the themes in primary debates but only 55% of the themes in general debates (see Table 9.1). This finding is consistent with previous research on primary versus general TV advertisements: 68% of the themes in primary TV spots are acclaims, whereas only 60% of the themes are acclaims in general TV spots (Benoit, 1999).

Given the fact that general debates have both more attacks and more defenses than primary debates, it is inevitable that they would have fewer acclaims. Conversely, primary debates, which have fewer attacks and fewer defenses, have more acclaims. There is a more positive tone to primary debates, and to primary spots, for that matter.

Less Emphasis on Policy in Primary Than General Debates

We compared the distribution of topics in primary and general debates (H8). Both campaign phases privilege policy. However, policy accounts for 63% of debate utterances in the primary campaign and 75% of debate comments in the general election. Of course, this means that character is stressed more in primary (37%) than general debates (25%). A chi-square calculated on topic in the two campaign phases was statistically significant (χ^2[df = 1] = 161.5, $p < .001$). These data are displayed in Table 9.3.

This same pattern occurs in primary and general television spots. Primary spots devote 52% of their remarks to policy, whereas general spots devote 60% of comments to policy (Benoit, 1999). Of course, character remarks decrease from 48% in the primary to 40% in the general campaign. A chi-square calculated on topics of primary and general TV spots was also significant (χ^2[df = 1] = 53.8, $p < .001$).

Earlier, we discussed the fact that, in general, candidates tend to discuss policy more than character and that this reflects the preferences of a majority of voters. However, in the primary, candidates are less well known than in the general campaign. First, the primary losers (e.g., in

2000, Bauer, Hatch, Keyes, and McCain) tend to be less well known than the winners (Bush, Gore). Second, even the winners are better known in the general campaign than in the primary. For example, voters knew more about George W. Bush in September or October of 2000 than they did in January or February of 2000. Thus, we can expect primary campaign messages to spend more time on introducing the candidates, on biographical or character concerns, than general campaign messages. Of course, there are some biographical TV spots in the fall; our argument is that there would be more emphasis on character in the winter and spring. Thus, it makes sense that presidential debates devote fewer themes to policy, and more themes to character, in the primary than the general campaign.

Fewer Past Deeds and More General Goals Occur in Primary Than General Debates

As predicted (H9), there is a difference in form of policy utterances between primary and general debates (χ^2[df = 2] = 311.0, $p < .001$). Inspection of Table 9.6 reveals that future plans remain about the same (24%, 23%). However, utterances on past deeds increase from primary to general debates (37%, 55%), whereas themes addressing general goals drop (40%, 21%). In general, we believe that nominees tend to have more executive experience than those who lose the primaries. Incumbents have, of course, served in the White House. Many other presidential nominees (primary winners) have been governors (like Reagan, Carter, Dukakis, Clinton, and George W. Bush) or vice presidents (like George H. W. Bush and Al Gore). While some unsuccessful primary candidates have experience in the House or Senate, that is not the same as executive experience. And other unsuccessful primary candidates (like Gary Bauer, Steve Forbes, Alan Keyes, Pat Buchanan) have even less government experience. This means that as a group the nominees who debate in the general election may have more executive experience than those who debate in primaries. This experience provides a greater basis for both acclaims and attacks on past deeds. Apparently, candidates in both phases want to show that they have some specific plans for action in office, which means that general goals are discussed more in primaries and are displaced in part by past deeds in the general debates.

Past Deeds Are Used to Attack More, and Acclaims Less, in Primary Than General Debates

The distribution of past deeds shifts by campaign phase (H10). Sixty-nine percent of past deeds are attacks and 31% are acclaims in the primary. Past deeds are composed of 59% attacks and 41% acclaims in the general campaign. This difference is significant (χ^2[df = 1] = 35.2, p < .001). See Table 9.6.

As noted above, we believe that candidates in the primary are, as a group, less likely to have executive experience than the nominees who compete in the general campaign. This means that many of these primary candidates have no past deeds in office to acclaim. However, attacks on past deeds are more common because they can attack both those opponents who do have experience in office and the other party. For example, Steve Forbes couldn't acclaim his experience as vice president or governor, but he could (and did) attack both George W. Bush and Bill Clinton. Similarly, McCain not only attacked Bush but also the Clinton/Gore administration's past deeds in the South Carolina debate: "Obviously we have too much deployment. We should have our troops coming home from Bosnia. We shouldn't have gone into Kosovo—or shouldn't have stumbled into Kosovo. There was no need to intervene there." Thus, we found that past deeds were used to attack more in the primary and to acclaim more in the general campaign.

Candidates Attack Their Own Party More Than the Other Party

We predicted that more attacks would be directed toward members of the party of the debate than toward members of the other party (H11). That is, in 2000 we expected Republicans Bauer, Bush, Forbes, Hatch, Keyes, and McCain to attack one another more than they would attack the Democrats (Gore or Bradley). In these debates, 1,082 attacks (47%) were directed toward members of one's own party, whereas 693 attacks (30%) targeted opposing party candidates (and 550, 24%, focused on the establishment) (see Table 9.8). Omitting attacks on the establishment (because they include members of both parties), a one-way chi-square confirmed this hypothesis (χ^2[df = 1] = 85.3, p < .001).

This finding makes sense despite Ronald Reagan's "eleventh commandment" against attacking one's own party. Members of the other party are not (yet) the opponent. No candidate in a contested primary can become president without first defeating the other contenders for the nomination of his or her own political party. Thus, in 2000, Bush had

TABLE 9.8
Target of Attack in Primary Debates

Own Party	Other Party	Establishment
1,082 (47%)	693 (30%)	550 (24%)

χ^2[df = 1] = 85.3, p < .001 for Own v. Other only

to defeat McCain (as well as the lesser threats, Bauer, Forbes, Hatch, and Keyes) before he could face Gore (or Bradley, if Bradley had won the Democratic nomination). Similarly, Bauer, Forbes, Hatch, Keyes, and McCain would have had to defeat Bush before they could have a real opportunity to face Gore as an opponent. The point of an attack is to achieve a net gain in favorability or preferability by reducing the favorability or preferability of one's opponent. Thus, when McCain attacks Bush (or vice versa) and succeeds in lowering the apparent desirability of that opponent, a drop in support for Bush helps McCain. For example, if McCain is at 40% in the polls and Bush is at 45%, an attack by McCain that dropped Bush's popularity to 35% would mean that McCain would take the lead. However, an attack by McCain on Gore (or Clinton/Gore) would not have the same effect: Bush, whom McCain must get past to face Gore, would still have a rating of 45% after McCain attacked Gore. Thus, in the primary there is more incentive, or more potential gain, from attacking one's immediate opponents than from attacking the opposition party.

Interestingly enough, when viewed from a certain perspective, attacks on the other party probably function to a certain extent somewhat like an acclaim. Again, assume that McCain is at 40% in the polls and Bush is at 45%. When McCain attacks Clinton/Gore, that attack may bolster his reputation among Republicans, say to 42% or 43%. Bush's popularity (or preferability) isn't damaged by McCain's attack on the Democrats, so he would remain at 45% in this hypothetical example. Thus, an effective attack against Gore could help McCain's popularity a bit among Republicans, but an effective attack against Bush could potentially gain him more ground. Strategically, McCain may be better advised to attack Bush than Gore (of course, there is always some risk of backlash against an attack).

More Attacks Target the Front-Runner Than Other Candidates

As predicted (H12), more attacks target the front-runner than other candidates. The front-runner, on average, received 16.2 attacks in these primary debates. Non-front-runners, again on average, received 5.7 attacks. Thus, front-runners are about three times more likely to be the target of an attack in primary debates than the other candidates. To test this relationship statistically, we correlated public opinion poll data with frequency of attack. To conduct this analysis we omitted debates in which there were only two opponents (for example, in 2000, Bradley and Gore had no other Democrats to attack besides each other) and debates in which the front-runner did not participate. Using Lexis-Nexis we located for each remaining debate a poll taken before the debate that asked voters to express a preference for a candidate. There is a significant positive correlation between a candidate's position in public opinion polls and the number of attacks targeted at that candidate in presidential primary debates ($r = .428$, $p < .001$, $N = 59$). The higher a candidate's standing in the polls, the more likely he or she is to be attacked in a primary debate. An r of .428 means that one's position in the polls accounts for almost 20% of the variance in target of attack.

This finding makes perfect sense. Everyone (else) trails the front-runner, so everyone benefits from attacks on the front-runner, which can increase their *net* favorability. For example, consider the following distribution of public support (data from a Gallup Poll reported in *USA Today* [2000]) for Republican candidates in January 2000:

Bush	63%
McCain	19%
Forbes	6%
Bauer	2%
Keyes	1%
Hatch	1%

Considering the race strategically, no candidate has much to gain from attacking Keyes or Hatch, both of whom are tied for dead last. If either of those two candidates could reduce Bauer's popularity, they could perhaps rise to a tie for fourth. Hatch, Keyes, and Bauer all have some reason to attack Forbes, because he is more likely to win the nomination than they are. Those candidates and Forbes have a reason to attack McCain. However, every other candidate has a strategic reason to attack Bush, because Bush will win the nomination as long as he maintains his lead. Thus, more candidates have strategic reasons to attack the front-runner than to attack anyone else. They have little strategic reason to attack those who are below them in the polls. Of course, they may have nonstrategic reasons to attack as well (perhaps they genuinely disagree on issues), but those kinds of attacks do not favor any particular candidate. Strategic considerations, however, are a reason to expect front-runners to be the target of most attacks—which they clearly receive.

Front-Runners Attack the Other Party More Than Other Candidates

We also expected that the front-running candidate would be more likely to attack the opposing party than other candidates (H13). This hypothesis was confirmed. Front-runners directed 51% of their attacks

toward the other party, whereas other candidates aimed only 37% of
their attacks at the other party. Another way to say this is that non-front-
runners devote 63% of their attacks to their own party, whereas front-
runners target only 49% of their attacks to fellow party members. A
chi-square calculated on target of attack from front-runners and other
candidates was significant (χ^2[df = 1] = 22.3, $p < .001$). See Table 9.9 for
these data.

These results are readily explicable. As just discussed, candidates
who trail the front-runner stand to gain by attacking the front-runner.
For example, if Forbes stood at 15% in the polls and Bush at 35%, any
reduction in Bush's popularity would bring Forbes that much closer to
winning the primaries. Forbes *has to* close the gap between himself and
Bush, or he will certainly lose the nomination. On the other hand, Bush
benefits less from attacks on Forbes, who already trails Bush in the polls.
Recall that if Bush attacks Forbes too vehemently, he risks alienating
Forbes and his supporters. On the other hand, this (alienation) is a haz-
ard that Forbes might be more willing to risk because he will definitely
lose if he cannot close the gap between them. Attacks from Bush on Gore
in the primary (or from Gore on Bush) may have somewhat of a benefi-
cial effect on fellow party members, functioning to a certain extent like
acclaims (as discussed earlier). Furthermore, if the front-runner succeeds at securing his (or her) party's nomination, attacks on the opposing party candidate during the primary may give a "jump-start" to that
candidate's general campaign. The front-runner, then, has less reason
than other candidates to attack members of his (or her) own party and
more (strategic) reason to attack the other party's candidates.

Thus, we found several findings that pertain to the primary campaign
phase. Candidates attack less often, and produce fewer defenses, in
primary than general debates. Although policy predominates in both
phases of the campaign, character is discussed more frequently in the
primary than the general campaign. Past deeds occur less often and
general goals more often in primary than general debates. When past
deeds do appear in debates, they are used to attack more, and acclaim
less, in primary than general debates. In general, candidates attack their

TABLE 9.9
**Target of Attacks in Primary Debates by Front-Runner vs. Other
Candidates**

Candidate	Own Party	Other Party
Front-Runner	181 (49%)	188 (51%)
Other Candidates	671 (63%)	393 (37%)

χ^2[df = 1] = 22.3, $p < .001$.

own party more than the other party (although front-runners attack the other party more than non-front-runners). More attacks are aimed at the front-runner than other candidates. As a group, primary debate candidates do not focus their comments on the issues that matter most to voters.

POLITICAL DEBATES

The campaign messages we studied here, of course, are political debates. We believe that debates have certain characteristics that distinguish them from other political messages. We made four specific predictions contrasting primary *debates* with primary *television spots* (because we have roughly comparable longitudinal data on primary spots). The results of our test of each hypothesis, along with a discussion of those results, will be presented in this section.

Defense Is More Frequent in Primary Debates Than TV Spots

As predicted (H14), primary debates included more defenses (4%) than primary TV spots (1%). A chi-square conducted on functions and primary message form was significant ($\chi^2[df = 2] = 150.8$, $p < .001$) (see Table 9.2). This result is consistent with previous research on the general campaign, which has found more defenses in general debates (Benoit, Blaney, & Pier, 1998; Benoit & Brazeal, in press; Benoit & Harthcock, 1999b; Benoit & Wells, 1996; Wells, 2000) than in general TV spots (Benoit, 1999).

We expect more defenses in debates than TV spots for two reasons. First, the candidate in a debate knows that the audience has heard the attack because attack and defense occur in the same message (in the same debate). Thus, unlike in TV spots, the candidate does not need to worry that he or she is informing or reminding the audience of an attack that they might have not heard or could have forgotten. Second, it is surely more difficult to resist the temptation to reply to an attack in the heat of a debate than in a scripted and rehearsed television spot. Thus, it is very reasonable to expect more defenses to occur in debates than in television spots—and that is just what we found.

Attacks Are More Frequent in Primary Debates Than TV Spots

Our hypothesis (H15), derived from comparisons of general debates and television spots, was not confirmed. Although the chi-square calculated on functions of primary message forms was significant (χ^2[df = 2] = 150.8, $p < .001$), attacks constituted 32% of primary debate utterances but only 28% of primary television spot themes (see Table 9.2). Thus, primary debates have more attacks than primary television spots.

It is not clear why primary messages (television spots and debates) do not follow the same pattern as general messages. As suggested earlier, it is possible that candidates are less well known in the primary than the general campaign. This would lead them to stress biographical television spots, which are more likely to contain attacks and acclaims. Of course, there are bio spots in general campaigns; however, we believe that there would be noticeably more bio spots in primary campaigns. If so, that could account for this unexpected finding.

Acclaims Are Less Frequent in Primary Debates Than TV Spots

This hypothesis (H16) was confirmed. Primary television spots employed more acclaims (71%) than primary debates (63%) (see Table 9.2; also Table 9.10). As indicated above, this chi-square was significant. Of course, if primary debates had more defenses and more attacks than primary television spots, as they in fact do, debates would have to employ fewer acclaims.

Debates Discuss Policy More (and Character Less) Than TV Spots

This hypothesis (H17) predicted that debates will discuss policy more than television spots. This hypothesis was confirmed (χ^2[df = 1] = 118.4, $p < .001$). Primary debates devote 63% of their utterances to policy and

TABLE 9.10
Functions of Political Campaign Discourse

Message Form	Function		
	Acclaims	Attacks	Defenses
Primary TV Spots	71%	28%	1%
Primary Debates	63%	32%	4%
Acceptance Addresses	72%	27%	1%
Keynote Speeches	51%	48%	1%
General TV Spots	60%	39%	1%
General Debates	55%	35%	10%

Data for acceptance addresses: Benoit, Wells, Pier, & Blaney, 2000. Date for television spots: Benoit, 1999; Benoit & Pier, 2000. Data for keynote speeches: Benoit, Blaney, & Pier, 2000. Data for debates: Benoit, Blaney, & Pier, 1998; Benoit & Brazeal, in press, Benoit & Harthcock, 1999b; Benoit & Wells, 1996; Wells, 1999.

37% to character (Table 9.4); general debates devote 75% of their comments to policy and 25% to character (Table 9.3); also see Table 9.11. A chi-square also finds that this relationship holds true in the general campaign as well (χ^2[df = 1] = 192.2, $p < .001$): TV spots focus less on policy in the primary (52%) than the general campaign (60%; see Benoit, 1999).

There could be several reasons for this finding. One major difference is that the candidates' utterances are constrained (at least in part) by the questions asked of them. It could be that the questions prompt the candidates to discuss their views on policy more than they do when making their television spots. Second, TV spots often need to introduce the candidates to voters, and so they may address biographical (character) topics more than debates. Thus, candidates tend to focus more on policy, and less on character, in debates than in television spots.

Our comparison of these two primary message forms revealed several differences between primary debates and primary television spots. Defense and attacks are more common in debates than spots, whereas acclaims are more common in television spots than debates. Finally, primary debates discuss policy more than primary television spots.

IMPLICATIONS

The primary phase is a very important part of our democratic process. It allows citizens to learn about the candidates and their policy positions. It allows political party members to determine who will be their party's nominee. This is a radical shift in presidential campaigns from even as recently as the 1960s when there were few primaries, and

TABLE 9.11
Topics in Political Campaign Discourse

Message Form	Topic	
	Policy	Character
Primary TV Spots	53%	47%
Primary Debates	63%	37%
Acceptance Addresses	56%	44%
Keynote Speeches	56%	44%
General TV Spots	60%	40%
General Debates	75%	25%

Data for acceptance addresses: Benoit, Wells, Pier, & Blaney, 1999. Data for television spots: Benoit, 1999; Benoit & Pier, 2000. Data for keynote speeches: Benoit, Blaney, & Pier, 2000. Data for debates: Benoit, Blaney, & Pier, 1998; Benoit & Brazeal, in press; Benoit & Harthcock, 1999b; Benoit & Wells, 1996; Wells, 1999.

primaries were not binding. In 1968, Hubert Humphrey won the Democratic nomination without campaigning in a single primary. The primary phase of the campaign has become more and more important in recent years.

This study has yielded a number of interesting conclusions. First, it demonstrates the utility of the Functional Theory of Political Campaign Discourse for analyzing campaign discourse. Of course, there are many questions this approach cannot answer (see, e.g., Hart's [2000] linguistic computer analysis of campaign messages). However, we believe it provides useful insights into campaign messages generally and into primary debates in particular.

Second, this research reinforces the important idea that presidential primary campaigns are different in important ways from general campaigns. These differences became manifest in these primary debates. For example, there are often multiple candidates participating in primary debates (inclusion of Perot in 1992 was unusual for general debates). This influences, for example, who is likely to be attacked. Front-runners are more likely to be the target of attacks than other candidates, and they tend to produce more defenses. Attacks provoke defenses, leaving less time for other functions.

Presidential primary campaigns can be a very important component of the campaign process. However, scholars lavish far more attention on the general phase of the campaign. This imbalance is an important concern precisely because primary campaigns differ in important (and may we add, significant) ways from general campaigns. Future research must work to redress this imbalance, increasing our knowledge of primary campaign discourse. Similarly, much more research has investigated general than primary presidential debates. Primary debates have the same advantages as general debates: They are longer than other message forms, like television spots; they offer a chance to compare the candidates side-by-side, generally addressing the same topics; and—while they do prepare for these encounters—debates are more spontaneous than other message forms, like scripted speeches or television spots, and hence may offer a somewhat more genuine view of the candidates. Thus, both the primary phase of the campaign generally and primary debates specifically merit further scholarly inquiry.

Appendix I

List of Primary Debates

Date	Location	Party	Participating Candidates
1948			
5/17	Portland, OR	R	Dewey, Stassen
1956			
5/21	Miami, FL	D	Kefauver, Stevenson
1960			
5/3	Charleston, WV	D	Humphrey, J. Kennedy
7/12	Los Angeles, CA	D	Johnson, J. Kennedy
1968			
6/1	San Francisco, CA	D	R. Kennedy, McCarthy
1972			
5/28	Burbank, CA	D	Humphrey, McGovern
5/30	Los Angeles, CA	D	Humphrey, McGovern
6/4	Los Angeles, CA	D	Chisholm, Hardin (for Wallace), Humphrey, McGovern, Yorty
1976			
2/23	Boston, MA	D	Bayh, Carter, Harris, H. Jackson, Shapp, Shriver, Udall

| 3/29 | New York, NY | D | Carter, Church, Harris, H. Jackson, Udall |
| 5/3 | Chicago, IL | D | Church, Udall |

1980

1/5	Des Moines, IA	R	Anderson, Baker, Bush, Connally, Crane, Dole
2/20	Manchester, NH	R	Anderson, Baker, Bush, Connally, Crane, Dole, Reagan
2/23	Nashua, NH	R	Bush, Reagan
2/28	Columbia, SC	R	Baker, Bush, Connally, Reagan
3/13	Chicago, IL	R	Anderson, Bush, Crane, Reagan
4/23	Grapevine, TX	R	Bush, Reagan

1984

1/15	Hanover, NH	D	Askew, Cranston, Glenn, Hart, Hollings, J. Jackson, McGovern, Mondale
1/31	Cambridge, MA	D	Cranston, Glenn, Hart, Hollings, J. Jackson, McGovern, Mondale
2/3	Boston, MA	D	Glenn, Hart, Hollings, J. Jackson, McGovern, Mondale
2/11	Des Moines, IA	D	Askew, Cranston, Glenn, Hart, Hollings, J. Jackson, McGovern, Mondale
2/23	Goffstown, NH	D	Askew, Cranston, Glenn, Hart, Hollings, J. Jackson, McGovern, Mondale
3/8	Atlanta, GA	D	Glenn, Hart, J. Jackson, McGovern, Mondale
3/18	Chicago, IL	D	Hart, J. Jackson, Mondale
3/28	New York, NY	D	Hart, J. Jackson, Mondale
4/5	Pittsburgh, PA	D	Hart, J. Jackson, Mondale
5/2	Grapevine, TX	D	Hart, J. Jackson, Mondale
6/3	Los Angeles, CA	D	Hart, J. Jackson, Mondale

1988

| 7/1 | Houston, TX | D | Biden, Babbitt, Dukakis, Gephardt, Gore, J. Jackson, Simon |
| 8/23 | Des Moines, IA | D | Biden, Babbitt, Dukakis, Gephardt, Gore, J. Jackson, Simon |

10/28	Houston, TX	R	Bush, Dole, DuPont, Haig, Kemp, Robertson
12/1	Washington, DC	D+R	Babbitt, Dukakis, Gephardt, Gore, J. Jackson, Simon, Bush, Dole, DuPont, Haig, Kemp, Robertson
1/8	Des Moines, IA	R	Bush, Dole, DuPont, Haig, Kemp, Robertson
1/15	Des Moines, IA	D	Babbitt, Dukakis, Gephardt, Gore, Hart, J. Jackson, Simon
1/16	Hanover, NH	R	Bush, Dole, DuPont, Haig, Kemp, Robertson
1/24	Durham, NH	D	Babbitt, Dukakis, Gephardt, Gore, Hart, J. Jackson, Simon
2/13	Goffstown, NH	D	Babbitt, Dukakis, Gephardt, Gore, Hart, J. Jackson, Simon
2/14	Concord, NH	R	Bush, Dole, Kemp, Robertson, DuPont
2/18	Dallas, TX	D	Dukakis, Gephardt, Gore, Hart, J. Jackson
2/19	Dallas, TX	R	Bush, Kemp
2/19	St. Paul, MN	D	Dukakis, Gephardt, J. Jackson, Simon
2/27	Atlanta, GA	D	Dukakis, Gephardt, Gore, Hart, J. Jackson, Simon
2/28	Atlanta, GA	R	Bush, Dole, Kemp, Robertson
2/29	Williamsburg, VA	D	Dukakis, Gephardt, Gore, Hart, J. Jackson
4/12	New York, NY	D	Dukakis, Gore, J. Jackson
4/17	New York, NY	D	Dukakis, Gore, J. Jackson
4/22	Philadelphia, PA	D	Dukakis, J. Jackson
4/23	Munhall, PA	D	Dukakis, J. Jackson
5/25	San Francisco, CA	D	Dukakis, J. Jackson

1992

12/15	Washington, DC	D	Brown, Clinton, Harkin, Kerrey, Tsongas, Wilder
1/19	Manchester, NH	D	Brown, Clinton, Harkin, Kerrey, Tsongas
1/31	Washington, DC	D	Brown, Clinton, Harkin, Kerrey, Tsongas

2/16	Goffstown, NH	D	Brown, Clinton, Harkin, Kerrey, Tsongas
2/23	Sioux Falls, SD	D	Agran, Brown, Clinton, Harkin, Kerrey, Tsongas
2/29	Denver, CO	D	Brown, Clinton, Harkin, Kerrey, Tsongas
3/1	Atlanta, GA	D	Brown, Clinton, Kerrey, Tsongas
3/1	College Park, MD	D	Brown, Clinton, Harkin, Tsongas
3/5	Dallas, TX	D	Brown, Clinton, Harkin, Tsongas
3/15	Chicago, IL	D	Brown, Clinton, Tsongas
3/27	St. Paul	D	Brown, Clinton
3/30	New York, NY	D	Brown, Clinton
4/5	New York, NY	D	Brown, Clinton
4/6	New York, NY	D	Brown, Clinton

1996

10/11	Manchester, NH	R	Alexander, Buchanan, Dole, Dornan, Forbes, Gramm, Keyes, Lugar, Spector, Taylor
1/6	Columbia, SC	R	Alexander, Buchanan, Gramm, Keyes, Lugar, Taylor
1/13	Johnston, IA	R	Alexander, Buchanan, Dole, Dornan, Forbes, Gramm, Keyes, Lugar, Taylor
2/15	Manchester, NH	R	Alexander, Buchanan, Dole, Dornan, Forbes, Keyes, Lugar, Taylor
2/22	Tempe, AZ	R	Alexander, Buchanan, Dornan, Forbes
2/29	Columbia, SC	R	Alexander, Buchanan, Dole, Forbes
3/3	Atlanta, GA	R	Alexander, Buchanan, Forbes

2000

10/22	Durham, NH	R	Bauer, Forbes, Hatch, Keyes, McCain
10/27	Hanover, NH	D	Bradley, Gore
10/28	Hanover, NH	R	Bauer, Forbes, Hatch, Keyes, McCain
11/21	Tempe, AZ	R	Forbes, Hatch, Keyes, McCain
12/2	Manchester, NH	R	Bauer, Bush, Forbes, Hatch, Keyes, McCain

12/6	Phoenix, AZ	R	Bauer, Bush, Forbes, Hatch, Keyes, McCain
12/13	Des Moines, IA	R	Bauer, Bush, Forbes, Hatch, Keyes, McCain
12/17	Nashua, NH	D	Bradley, Gore
12/19	Washington, DC	D	Bradley, Gore
1/5	Durham, NH	D	Bradley, Gore
1/6	Durham, NH	R	Bauer, Bush, Forbes, Hatch, Keyes, McCain
1/7	Lexington, SC	R	Bauer, Bush, Forbes, Hatch, Keyes, McCain
1/8	Johnston, IA	D	Bradley, Gore
1/10	Grand Rapids, MI	R	Bauer, Bush, Forbes, Hatch, Keyes, McCain
1/15	Johnston, IA	R	Bauer, Bush, Forbes, Hatch, Keyes, McCain
1/17	Des Moines, IA	D	Bradley, Gore
1/26	Manchester, NH	R	Bauer, Bush, Forbes, Keyes, McCain
1/26	Manchester, NH	D	Bradley, Gore
2/15	Columbia, SC	R	Bush, Keyes, McCain
2/21	New York, NY	D	Bradley, Gore
3/1	Los Angeles, CA	D	Bradley, Gore
3/2	Los Angeles, CA	R	Bush, Keyes, McCain

Appendix II
Sample Acclaims and Attacks on Forms of Policy and Character

POLICY

Past Deeds
> *Acclaim*: "I've actually worked on long-term care issues from the time I was in the Senate. I'm one of the prime authors of the home health care bill." (Hatch)
> *Attack*: "We've been closing veterans' hospitals around the country and that's outrageous." (Bauer)

Future Plans
> *Acclaim*: "I will repeal most favored nation status for China." (Bauer)
> *Attack*: "Governor Bush's plan has not one penny for Social Security, not one penny for Medicare, and not one penny for paying down the national debt." (McCain)

General Goals
> *Acclaim*: "I want to reform education and the military and health care and the tax code. We can't do that unless we get the government out of the hands of the special interests and back into the public interests." (McCain)
> *Attack*: Both Democratic candidates support "The idea that the federal government should make all decisions for consumers and the federal government should make all decisions for the provider, that the federal government should ration care." (Bush)

CHARACTER

Personal Qualities

Acclaim: Two important traits are "faithfulness and fidelity to ideas and promises. You can depend on me." (Forbes)

Attack: "I speak about the deceit and corruption of this administration." (Hatch)

Leadership Ability

Acclaim: "One of the things I've learned as the governor of Texas is that if you set a clear enough agenda . . . and you know how to bring people together to achieve an agenda, things can get done." (Bush)

Attack: "I'm worried about the country. I'm worried about whether or not we're going to have a continuation of the present leadership. I really want to see the Clinton-Gore team go." (Hatch)

Ideals

Acclaim: "I see, like you, great possibilities for America—what Abraham Lincoln called a 'new birth of freedom.' Whether it's the freedom to be born, freedom from fear of the IRS, freedom to choose your own schools, freedom to choose your own doctors, freedom to be in charge of your own health care, freedom to be safe and secure in this world." (Forbes)

Attack: "Bill Clinton's not the only one who needs to shape up. We all need to shape up, starting with getting back to our allegiance to the fundamental moral principles that are this nation's strength and that ought to shape its heart." (Keyes)

References

Abramson, P. R., Aldrich, J. H., & Rohde, D. W. (1982). *Change and continuity in the 1980 elections*. Washington: Congressional Quarterly, Inc.

Allis, S. (1992, March 30). Broke but unbowed. *Time, 139*, 26.

Barrett, L. I. (1992a, January 27). Nipping at Clinton's heels. *Time, 139*, 22–23.

Barrett, L. I. (1992b, February 17). Tsongas' surprising surge. *Time, 139*, 23.

Benoit, P. J. (1997). *Telling the success story: Acclaiming and disclaiming discourse*. Albany: State University of New York Press.

Benoit, W. L. (1995). *Accounts, excuses, and apologies: A theory of image restoration strategies*. Albany: State University of New York Press.

Benoit, W. L. (1999). *Seeing spots: A functional analysis of presidential television advertisements from 1952–1996*. Westport, CT: Praeger.

Benoit, W. L., Blaney, J. R., & Pier, P. M. (1998). *Campaign '96: A functional analysis of acclaiming, attacking, and defending*. Westport, CT: Praeger.

Benoit, W. L., Blaney, J. R., & Pier, P. M. (2000). Acclaiming, attacking, and defending: A functional analysis of nominating convention keynote speeches, 1960–1996. *Political Communication, 17*, 61–84.

Benoit, W. L., & Brazeal, L. M. (in press). A functional analysis of the 1988 Bush–Dukakis presidential debates. *Argumentation and Advocacy*.

Benoit, W. L., & Dorries, B. (1996). *Dateline NBC*'s persuasive attack on Wal-Mart. *Communication Quarterly, 44*, 464–477.

Benoit, W. L., & Harthcock, A. (1999a). Attacking the tobacco industry: A rhetorical analysis of advertisements by the The Campaign for Tobacco-Free Kids. *Southern Communication Journal, 65*, 66–81.

Benoit, W. L., & Harthcock, A. (1999b). Functions of the Great Debates: Acclaims, attacks, and defense in the 1960 presidential debates. *Communication Monographs, 66*, 341–357.

Benoit, W. L., McKinney, M. S., & Stephenson, M. T. (in press). Effects of watching campaign 2000 presidential primary debates. *Journal of Communication*.

Benoit, W. L., Pier, P. M., & Blaney, J. R. (1997). A functional approach to televised political spots: Acclaiming, attacking, and defending. *Communication Quarterly, 45*, 1–20.

Benoit, W. L., & Stephenson, M. T. (2000). *Effects of watching a presidential primary debate.* Unpublished manuscript.

Benoit, W. L., & Wells, W. T. (1996). *Candidates in conflict: Persuasive attack and defense in the 1992 presidential debates.* Tuscaloosa: University of Alabama Press.

Benoit, W. L., Wells, W. T., Pier, P. M., & Blaney, J. R. (1999). Acclaiming, attacking, and defending in nomination convention acceptance addresses, 1960-1996. *Quarterly Journal of Speech, 85*, 247–267.

Berelson, B. (1952). *Content analysis for the social sciences and humanities.* Reading, MA: Addison-Wesley.

Berquist, G. F. (1960). The Kennedy-Humphrey debate. *Today's Speech, 8*, 2–3, 31.

Best, S. J., & Hubbard, C. (2000). The role of televised debates in the presidential nominating process. In W. G. Mayer (Ed.), *In pursuit of the White House 2000: How we choose our presidential nominees* (pp. 255–284). New York: Chatham House.

Blankenship, J., Fine, M. G., & Davis, L. K. (1983). The 1980 Republican primary debates: The transformation of actor to scene. *Quarterly Journal of Speech, 64*, 25–36.

Brinkley, A. (1995). *American history: A survey.* St. Louis: McGraw-Hill.

Brookhiser, R. (1986). *The outside story: How Democrats and Republicans re-elected Reagan.* Garden City, NY: Doubleday.

CBS News/*New York Times.* (1980a, February 13). Poll. Accession number 0015172; Question number 029. *http://web.lexis-nexis.com/universe.* [Accessed 5/12/01].

CBS News/*New York Times.* (1980b, September 10). Poll. Accession number 0018361; Question number 022. *http://web.lexis-nexis.com/universe.* [Accessed 5/12/01].

CBS News/*New York Times.* (1984, April 23). Poll. Accession number 0016338; Question number 004. *http://web.lexis-nexis.com/universe.* [Accessed 5/12/01].

CNN/*USA Today.* (1992, January 3). Poll. Accession number 0167507, Question number 019. *http://web.lexis-nexis.com/universe.* [Accessed 5/14/01].

Cambridge Reports. (1988, February). Poll. *http://web.lexis-nexis.com/universe.* [Accessed 5/12/01].

Carlin, D. B. (1994). A rationale for a focus group study. In D. B. Carlin & M. S. McKinney (Eds.) *The 1992 presidential debates in focus* (pp. 3–19). Westport, CT: Praeger.

Carlin, D. B., & McKinney, M. S. (Eds.). (1994). *The 1992 presidential debates in focus.* Westport, CT: Praeger.

Carlson, M. (1992, March 23). Why Jerry keeps running. *Time, 139*, 27.

Center for Responsive Politics. (1988). *Beyond the 30-second spot: Enhancing the media's role in congressional campaigns.* Washington: CRP.

Church, G. J. (1992, February 24). Will someone else leap in? *Time, 139*, 22–23.

Clinton's message. (1992, March 21). *The Economist, 322*, 13–14.

Cohen, J. (1960). A coefficient of agreement for nominal scales. *Educational and Psychological Measurement, 20*, 37–46.

Collins, S. D. (1986). *The Rainbow challenge: The Jackson campaign and the future of U.S. politics*. New York: Monthly Review Press.

Coolidge, D. A. (1990). The Revered Jesse Jackson and the Palestinian question. In L. Morris (Ed.), *The social and political implications of the 1984 Jesse Jackson presidential campaign*. Westport, CT: Praeger.

Davis, J. W. (1997). Primary debates. In *U.S. presidential primaries and the caucus-convention system: A sourcebook* (pp. 146–156). Westport, CT: Praeger.

The fine old contest that could be. (1992, March 14). *The Economist, 322*, 25–26.

Fleiss, J. L. (1981). *Statistical methods for ratios and proportions*. New York: Wiley.

From sea to shining sea. (1992, February 15). *The Economist, 322*, 25–26.

Gallup. (1992, January 14). Accession number 0167507, Question number 019. *http://www.lexis-nexis.com/universe* [Accessed 4/8/00].

Germond, J. W., & Witcover, J. (1985). *Wake us when it's over: Presidential politics of 1984*. New York: Macmillan.

Heartburn in the heartland. (1992, February 29). *The Economist, 322*, 26–27.

Hellweg, S. A., Pfau, M., & Brydon, S. R. (1992). *Televised presidential debates: Advocacy in contemporary America*. Westport, CT: Praeger.

Hellweg, S.A., & Phillips, S.L. (1981). A verbal and visual analysis of the 1988 Houston Republican presidential primary debate. *Southern Speech Communication Journal, 47*, 23–38.

Henry, W. A. (1985). *Visions of America: How we saw the 1984 election*. Boston: Atlantic Monthly Press.

Hinck, E. A. (1993). *Enacting the presidency: Political argument, presidential debates, and presidential character*. Westport, CT: Praeger.

Holbrook, T. M. (1996). *Do campaigns matter?* Thousand Oaks, CA: Sage.

Holsti, O. (1952). *Content analysis in communication research*. New York: Free Press.

Holsti, O.R. (1969). *Content analysis for the social sciences and humanities*. Reading, MA: Addison-Wesley.

Hull, J. D. (1992, March 30). Sweet smell of success. *Time, 139*, 20–25.

Jamieson, K. H. (1987). Television, presidential campaigns, and debates. In J. L. Swerdlow (Ed.), *Presidential debates 1988 and beyond* (pp. 27–33). Washington: Congressional Quarterly Inc.

Jamieson, K. H. (1996). *Packaging the presidency: A history and criticism of presidential campaign advertising*. (3rd ed.) New York: Oxford University Press.

Jamieson, K. H., & Birdsell, D. S. (1988). *Presidential debates: The challenge of creating an informed electorate*. New York: Oxford University Press.

Joslyn, R. A. (1980). The content of political spot ads. *Journalism Quarterly, 57*, 92–98.

Kane, T. (1987). The Dewey-Stassen primary debate of 1948: An examination of format for presidential debates. In J. Wenzel (Ed.), *Argument and critical practices* (pp. 249–253). Annandale, VA: Speech Communication Association.

Kendall, K. E. (2000). *Communication in the presidential primaries: Candidates and the media, 1912–2000*. Westport, CT: Praeger.

Kraus, S. (Ed.). (1979). *The great debates: Carter versus Ford 1976*. Bloomington: Indiana University Press.

Lanoue, D. J., & Schrott, P. R. (1989). Voters' reactions to televised presidential debates: Measurement of the source and magnitude of opinion change. *Political Psychology, 10,* 275–285.

Lenart, S. (1994). *Shaping political attitudes: The impact of interpersonal communication and mass media.* Thousand Oaks, CA: Sage.

Levine, M.A. (1995). *Presidential campaigns and elections: Issues and images in the media age,* 2nd ed. Itasea, IL: Peacock.

Maisel, L. S. (1999). *Parties and elections in America,* (3rd ed.) Oxford, UK: Rowman & Littlefield.

Mann, T. E. (1985). Elected officials and the politics of presidential selection. In A. Ranney (Ed.), *The American elections of 1984* (pp. 100–128). Durham, NC: Duke University Press.

Mansfield, H. C. (1987). The 1984 election: Entitlements versus opportunity. In P. E. Schramm & D. J. Mahoney (Eds.), *The 1984 Election and the future of American politics* (pp. 277–288). Durham, NC: Carolina Academic Press.

Martel, M. (1983). *Political campaign debates: Images, strategies, and tactics.* New York: Longman.

Merritt, S. (1984). Negative political advertising: Some empirical findings. *Journal of Advertising, 13,* 27–38.

Moody Michigan. (1992, March 14). *The Economist, 322,* 26.

Morris, L. (1990). The range and limits of campaign politics. In L. Morris (ed.), *The social and political implications of the 1984 Jesse Jackson presidential campaign* (pp. 3–13). Westport, CT: Praeger.

Murphy, J. M. (1992). Presidential debates and campaign rhetoric: Text within context. *Southern Communication Journal, 57,* 219–228.

Nelson, M. (Ed.). (1989). Candidate debates. In *Congressional Quarterly's guide to the presidency.* Washington: Congressional Quarterly.

O'Keefe, D. J. (1977). Two concepts of argument. *Journal of the American Forensic Association, 13,* 121–128.

Orren, G. R. (1985). The nomination process: Vicissitudes of candidate selection. In M. Nelson (Ed.), *The elections of 1984* (pp. 27–82). Washington: Congressional Quarterly.

Page, H. F. (1990). Lessons of the Jackson campaign: Discursive strategies and symbolic control and cultural capitalization. In L. Morris (Ed.), *The social and political implications of the 1984 Jesse Jackson presidential campaign.* Westport, CT: Praeger.

Pfau, M. (1984). A comparative assessment of intra-party political debate formats. *Political Communication Review, 8,* 1–23.

Pfau, M. (1987). The influence of intraparty debates on candidate preference. *Communication Research, 14,* 687–697.

Pfau, M. (1988). Intra-party political debates and issue learning. *Journal of Applied Communication Research, 16,* 99–112.

Pomper, G. M. (1981). The nominating contests. (1–37). In G. M. Pomper (Ed.). *The election of 1980: Reports and interpretations.* Chatham, NJ: Chatham House Publishers, Inc.

Popkin, S. L. (1994). *The reasoning voter: Communication and persuasion in presidential campaigns.* Chicago: University of Chicago Press.

Princeton Survey Research Associates. (1999, October 7). Poll. Accession number 0341860, Question number 049. *http://web.lexis-nexis.com/universe*. [Accessed 5/14/01].

Ray, R. F. (1961). Thomas E. Dewey: The great Oregon debate of 1948. In R. Reid (Ed.), *American public address: Studies in honor of Albert Craig Baird* (pp. 245–270). Columbia: University of Missouri Press.

Rueter, T. (1983). *Transcripts of the 1980 presidential debates*. Ann Arbor, MI: University Microfilm.

Royer, C. T. (ed.) (1994). *Campaign for president: The managers look at '92*. Hollis, NH: Hollis Publishing.

Smith, C. A. (1990). *Political communication*. San Diego: Harcourt Brace Jovanovich.

Splaine, J. (1995). *The road to the White House since television*. Washington: S-SPAN.

Stelzner, H. G. (1971). Humphrey and Kennedy court West Virginia, May 3, 1960. *Southern Speech Communication Journal, 37,* 21–33.

Stewart, C. J. (1975). Voter perception of mud-slinging in political communication. *Central States Speech Journal, 26,* 279–286.

Stone, W. J., Rapoport, R. B., & Abramowitz, A.I. (1989). *The Reagan revolution and party polarization in the 1980s*. Paper presented at the annual meeting of the American Political Science Association.

Swerdlow, J. L. (1984). *Beyond debate: A paper on televised presidential debates*. New York: Twentieth Century Fund.

Swerdlow, J. L. (1987). *Presidential debates 1988 and beyond*. Washington: Congressional Quarterly Inc.

Thurow, G. E. (1987). The 1984 Democratic primary election: Issues and image. In P. E. Schramm & D. J. Mahoney (Eds.), *The 1984 election and the future of American politics* (pp. 37–52). Durham, NC: Carolina Academic Press.

Trent, J. S., & Friedenberg, R. V. (2000). *Political campaign communication: Principles and practices*, 4/e. Westport, CT: Praeger.

Walters, R. W. (1990). The issue politics of the Jesse Jackson campaign for president in 1984. In L. Morris (Ed.), *The social and political implications of the 1984 Jesse Jackson presidential campaign* (pp. 15–48). Westport, CT: Praeger.

Wattenberg, M.P. (1986). The Reagan polarization phenomenon and the continuing downward slide in presidential candidate popularity. *American Politics Quarterly, 14,* 219–245.

Wells, W.T. (2000). *An analysis of attacking, acclaiming, and defending strategies in the 1976–1984 presidential debates*. Ph.D. dissertation University of Missouri, Columbia.

West, D. M. (1997). *Air wars: Television advertising in election campaigns 1952–1996* (2d ed.) Washington: Congressional Quarterly.

Wormser, M. D. (1984). *Campaign '84*. Washington: Congressional Quarterly.

Yawn, M., Ellsworth, K., Beatty, B., & Kahn, K. F. (1998). How a presidential primary debate changed attitudes of audience members. *Political Behavior, 20,* 155–181.

Subject Index

Author Index

ABOUT THE AUTHORS

WILLIAM L. BENOIT is Professor of Communication at the University of Missouri. Benoit has published extensively in political communication, including *The Clinton Scandals and the Politics of Image Restoration*, with Joseph R. Blaney (Praeger, 2001).

P. M. PIER is with the Department of Communication at the University of Missouri. In addition to *Campaign '96: A Functional Analysis of Acclaiming, Attaching, and Defending*, with William L. Benoit and Joseph R. Blaney (Praeger, 1998), she has published in *Argumentation and Advocacy*.

LEANN M. BRAZEAL is with the Department of Communication at the University of Missouri. She has published in *Argumentation and Advocacy*.

JOHN P. McHALE is with the Department of Communication at the University of Missouri. He has published in *Communication Quarterly* and *Critical Studies in Media Communication*.

ANDREW KLYUKOVSKI is with the Department of Communication at the University of Missouri. He has published in *Critical Studies in Media Communication*.

DAVID AIRNE is with the Department of Communication at the University of Missouri. He has published in *Critical Studies in Media Communication*.